LIVERPOOL
GATEWAY of EMPIRE

TONY LANE

LAWRENCE & WISHART
✴
LONDON

Lawrence and Wishart Limited
39 Museum Street
London WC1A 1LQ

First published 1987

Photoset in North Wales by
Derek Doyle & Associates, Mold, Clwyd
Printed in Great Britain by
Oxford University Press

For Kevin

Contents

Preface

Encounters with Liverpudlians followed by enquiries about their families lead to the sea lanes of the world. So many people from this city were once crew members of merchant ships that almost everyone can find a seafaring relative. Struggling with the first chapter of this book and temporarily escaped, my car broke down outside a mid-nineteenth-century pub. The Pontack, named after a tribe of North American Indians, itself suggested Atlantic voyages, and conversation with the landlady soon revealed a connection. Once at sea as a stewardess, she proudly told me how she had sailed on the *Queen Mary*'s last voyage, round Cape Horn to Long Beach, California.

In Liverpool the sea cannot be avoided. All the arterial roads to the city converge on the river at the Pierhead. The main streets collect the prevailing southwesterlies and send them swirling past shop and office windows. Standing outside the Town Hall and looking down Water Street at high tide, inward and outward bound ships move across the frame made by the Cunard and Liver Buildings.

A Southerner from the Isle of Wight, I first arrived in

Liverpool in the late spring of 1955 to be interviewed by the marine superintendant of Ellerman Hall Lines for an apprenticeship. Turned down, it was almost a year before I returned. This time, like millions before me and after me, I came by sea. It was the end of my first voyage. Home from Australia and with the ship's belly full of meat and wool, we had almost a week in Liverpool before going round to London to pay off.

On my first run ashore I took the overhead railway which followed the line of the docks at a height just above the top of the massive granite dock wall. Looking down into the docks I was as amazed and delighted as every other novice to Liverpool. There were a lot of strange ships with cargoes smelling a good deal stronger than anything on my ship. Already, after only five months at sea, I reckoned that this was my world. After another eight years or so I changed my mind about seafaring – but never about Liverpool. Like many other seafarers I believed – but without thinking about it that way – that Liverpool was the place that most perfectly expressed ships and seafaring. This was a port that bundled everything together that was to do with ships and captured the jokes and joking relationships, the carpings, anxieties, tragedies and hardships that make up the solidarity of seafaring.

Liverpool was a sailors' city like no other, although by the 1950s the port had long passed its peak and by then there were other and greater ports than Liverpool in the world (although this wasn't something that a sensible Southerner would say to a Liverpudlian). Hamburg and Rotterdam, Valparaiso and San Francisco, Hong Kong and Yokohama all featured in sailors' legends and each had its dedicated band of followers. But where these cities had their special districts for visiting seafarers, the sailors' haunts in Liverpool were never so concentrated – and here in this city it was as if ships entered its very heart. The river sounds were scored into those of the streets and the tram and bus terminus was within heaving-line distance of passenger ships bound for every continent except Europe. Liverpool looked outward, not over its shoulder.

Amongst Liverpool residents there were thousands who were at sea on ships and tens of thousands who had once been to sea and who on the first warm day of spring and the first drear day of winter dreamed of going back 'for just one more trip'. There were also further thousands of children and adolescents who would unquestionably follow their brothers and cousins, fathers and uncles – and even handfuls who would follow sisters and aunts. Among this multitude, visiting seafarers found, as I did, a population who seemed to be understanding members of the same family.

I found Liverpool a warm and welcoming place. I loved the city streets which opened to the river and the brass plates announcing ocean connections. I loved the blunt self-confidence of the people who would claim a stranger as a fellow member of the human race. I loved the anarchic, good-humoured mockery of a people who refused to be servile and defiantly guarded their independence. I think I quickly noticed this social character that has made Liverpool such a decidedly distinctive place, but thirty years ago I was far too young and ignorant to begin to understand what had formed the city and its people. I knew only that I felt more at home here than anywhere else I had ever been. I am still discovering Liverpool but, at last, I feel confident enough to try to explain its unique character to others who have not had my opportunity of living and working in one of Western Europe's most fascinating cities.

I cannot begin to acknowledge properly all the

friends, acquaintances and people of chance encounters in streets, shops, offices, pubs, buses, trains,
waiting rooms, park benches, cinema queues and the
river-watchers at the Pierhead who have taught me
about Liverpool. There are also all those people in local
government offices and libraries who, over many many
years, have guided me to new sources of information.
But I can at least thank Pat Hudson who, in the
writing of this book, has been my sternest critic and
strongest friend. Thanks are also due to Matt Simpson
for permission to quote from his poems. Trevor
Skempton who drew the illustrations is an old friend
and fellow admirer of Liverpool. He produced his
highly distinctive and original drawings at very short
notice and I hope readers will be as delighted with
them as I am. Finally, there are Trish McMillan and Di
Murgatroyd who typed my manuscript and are an
unforgettable pair of colleagues. I need only step into
their office to be confronted with the real democratic
temper of Liverpool.

Tony Lane
July 1987

Introduction

In 1982 a *Daily Mirror* reporter wrote:

> They should build a fence around [Liverpool] and charge admission. For sadly, it has become a 'showcase' of everything that has gone wrong in Britain's major cities.[1]

Liverpool is the only city in Britain (apart from London) upon which other Britons have definite opinions and it is seen as a city of problems where the people themselves are reckoned to be part of the problem. This book, through an exploration of Liverpool's modern history, explains why this city has become the object of so much interest in Britain and Europe over the last two decades.

In the clamour of argument about cities, about city
life and city people that has continued unabated since
the eighteenth century, Liverpool's prominence is
recent. In the nineteenth century Manchester and Salford were held to exemplify best the horrors of indus-
trialisation, and the London working classes were
thought to be the most turbulent and threatening in
England. For most of the twentieth century Glasgow
has provided the model of overcrowding, urban dere-
liction and violent crime. In the case of the cities just
mentioned, each represented the anxieties characteris-
tic of a particular period. In the late twentieth century it
has been Liverpool's turn to be presented as containing
a distilled essence of the 'British problem'. And it was
Liverpool's misfortune to acquire this symbolic status
in a period when television technology reached matur-
ity and when the popular press had become ever more
stridently propagandist.

Liverpool has had the high statistics of unemployment, the numerical and visible evidence of an
impoverished city treasury, a sufficiently large number
of deserted factories sporting 'For Sale' and 'To Let'
boards hanging awry and faded by sun and weather, the
slogans of disaffection and demoralisation aerosoled
over boarded up shop-fronts on suburban council
estates. But in themselves these are not sufficient
reasons for focusing on Liverpool. There are other large
towns with more people out of work, towns with worse
housing conditions, other towns with higher strike
rates and many cities far worse for street and violent
crime. The attraction of Liverpool for the news media is
not that the city has more of the 'bad' things than
anywhere else, it is the amalgam of problems and the
general familiarity with the place and its people
through the products of popular culture – rock music,
football, soap operas, comedians.

Liverpool has also provided a series of incidents, events and personalities that have continuously seemed appropriate to the time and the moment. The car industry arrived when the industrial relations of car-making were everywhere undergoing upheaval; the docks, more important to the life of the city than any other industry, were being transformed at the same time as the industry *worldwide* was being turned upside down and similarly racked by unrest. Cars and docks were enough, when combined in one city, to give Liverpool a reputation for trade union militancy that it had never had before. Simultaneously, working-class life had now become an acceptable dramatic location and Liverpool in the 1960s was home for a new generation of working-class playwrights who could get their scripts accepted in Sir Hugh Greene's BBC and Sidney Bernstein's Granada. From the early 1960s until the mid-1970s it did seem as if the archaic, class-encrusted attitudes and institutions of Britain's dominant classes were at last being deposed. Liverpool, with its defiant and ready-witted people, seemed to express it all.

One of the most striking characteristics of Liverpool people is their democratic inclination. This does not express itself in such an ordinary thing as an exceptionally high voting turn-out at elections but in the way the people think, feel and act. The inclination shows in the way Liverpudlians will talk confidently and unselfconsciously on equal terms with others regardless of their status; it shows, too, in their cheerful readiness to mock and puncture pretension. But it shows more than anywhere else in a cavalier disregard for money. This is a city with the habit of the seafarer ashore after a voyage – spend it while you can because the world might end tomorrow. Strangers quickly sense the large spendthrift generosity of

Liverpool, for they cannot help but notice the astonishing number of London-style black cabs on the streets. Indeed the cabs should be referred to as Liverpool-style for where in the Metropolitan Police District of London there is one cab for every 522 persons, in Liverpool there is one for every 360. Manchester has a different outlook on life for it has one cab for every 997 persons. Such an elementary statistic encodes the particularity of Liverpool.

This book is preoccupied with exploring the dimensions and explaining the genesis of Liverpool's social character. There is, however, another aspect of this matter which, although not developed in the text, should be mentioned – it is the tangled question of the extent to which Britain can be understood as one nation.

The politics of Northern Ireland and the persistence of nationalist parties in Scotland and Wales have already contributed to the unravelling of the idea of Britain as a place with a cultural unity. The last two sets of General Election results and the rediscovery of ideas of regional and decentralised government by the centre and the left of politics have prompted a renewal of the debate on the proper structure of the modern nation state.

Social historians have for long suspected that underneath the idea of the nation there lay a fair amount of diversity that had by no means been swamped by the economic and political developments of the nineteenth century. It is impossible not to be impressed by the internal migration statistics which show that most changes of residence take place over very short distances – and then to discover from everyday encounters that very large numbers of people seem hardly ever to travel and so live out their lives in restricted milieux.

When Asa Briggs wrote his famous *Victorian Cities*

the view was that although the great cities of the nineteenth century often had their own distinctive characters this separateness did not last very long:

> During the 1890s the pull of London tightened. Local newspapers began to lose ground to national newspapers. National advertising began to increase greatly in scope and scale. The same branded goods began to be offered in shops in all parts of the country. Neither the aesthete nor the expert was as much at home in the provinces as he was in the huge metropolis. Political and economic trends began to depend less on local social and market forces and more on national pressures from the centre. It was then, as the same kind of working-class houses were being built in the same kind of suburbs ... that cities began to be more alike ...[2]

In these remarks there is a lot to agree with, and since Briggs wrote them the further growth of national and international firms has hastened the homogenising process. In Britain, more than anywhere else in Western Europe, towns and cities have the same shops selling the same goods at the same prices, and no other country is so densely served with national media of communication. But does it follow that because the British population buys the same sort of commodities and consumes the same media that it everywhere becomes the same or very similar in outlook and disposition? The view which is at first so plausible is in fact deeply flawed.

Even in terms of consumption there are some marked regional variations. But where the real differences emerge is in the area of economic production. Every city tends to employ the same proportions of its population in retailing, in transport and communication, in financial services, in building and construction, but what distinguishes one from the other and gives each its own character is the branch or branches of industry in which it specialises and has specialised. Cities are a bit like nation states. Unable to produce for all their needs, they have to engage in external trade. Since the de-industrialisation which has hit many cities during the last two decades it is not so obvious what differentiates, say, Manchester from Liverpool. But the answer was plain enough in 1901 – Liverpool imported the cotton which Manchester then spun and wove. Liverpool, by virtue of being a port, and Manchester, by virtue of being a cotton town, were very different places. The one city required a large and casually employed population to sail the ships, repair them, load, discharge, store, shift and process their cargoes. When the ships were in, many might work; when the docks were slack, workers were laid off. Seasons, weather and tide affected the economy of Liverpool to an extent scarcely felt by the more regularly employed factory workers of Manchester. And then Liverpool also had a continuously transient population of seafarers to give it colour, variety and cosmopolitanism. It was being a port city on a scale unseen anywhere else in Britain that made Liverpool such a particular place. In its ethos, if not in its employment statistics, that was almost as true in 1961 and even 1981 as it had been in 1901. The economic pattern laid down in the nineteenth century sealed the social character of many British cities and of Liverpool in particular.

City inhabitants know their cities in ways that they cannot possibly know their nation – the experience of the one is as immediate and direct as the experience of the other is indeterminate and indirect. And so despite a common language, a common legal system, national myths, national heroes and a national anthem, the experience of being British is not everywhere the same.

Citizens' loyalties are first engaged by the particular-ities of their cities which shape and form their attitudes. 'Britishness' is what everyone has in common *after* they are Liverpudlians, Mancunians, Bristolians or whatever ... and is probably more important to people who live in villages and small towns which are too limited in their functions to generate a particular social character and are, therefore, more dependent upon an association with the emblems and symbols of Britishness. This is to stand conventional distinctions between small towns and cities on their head, for it suggests that it is city dwellers who are the most locally oriented and the most 'parochial'.

Local identifications permeate all sections of a city's population – but not all of them equally. Middle-class people are not ordinarily enthusiastic about their children acquiring whatever is the local accent and this in itself is a sure indication that *their* horizons extend beyond the city. Middle-class people are those who are most residentially mobile over long distances because they are oriented toward progress through a hierarchy of occupation or profession. Working-class people, by contrast, have little expectation of progress in a career and generally expect to live out their lives in one place. This is confirmed by the facts of residential mobility.[3] Differences in rates of mobility suggest that whatever the social character which attaches to cities, the particularity of it is most likely to be the product of working-class life and working-class institutions.

Regardless of the extent to which different social classes contribute to the social character of the modern city, and in spite of the undoubted levelling processes at work in the twentieth century, other economic and social forces have ensured the survival of powerful identifications with city and city-region. This is important and encouraging. A flourishing democracy needs citizens who can identify and, through identification, participate.

Notes

1 *Daily Mirror*, 11 October 1982.
2 Asa Briggs, *Victorian Cities*, Harmondsworth 1968, p.48.
3 See A.I. Harris and R. Clausen, *Labour Mobility in Great Britain*, London 1966. Indicative is the finding that 71 per cent of those with a university education had moved at least once in the previous ten years compared with 47 per cent of those with secondary modern education.

1 Gateway of Empire

Cities with national and international reputations are recognised through a symbolic building. Where New York is the Empire State Building and Paris the Eiffel Tower, Liverpool is the Royal Liver Building. Sometimes loathed by architectural critics for its vulgarity – 'swagger though coarse', says Pevsner – painters, poster artists and television producers needing an instantly recognisable image of Liverpool nevertheless have the building somewhere in frame.[1]

When the Liver Building was opened in 1910 its clock mechanisms were boastfully presented as being the largest of their kind. By way of underlining such a trivial fact, the Royal Liver directors ate dinner off one of the clockfaces before it was put in place. That

flamboyant gesture was of a piece with the times and
the assertiveness that was even then so characteris-
tically Liverpool.

The city was at its peak in 1910. Victoria, only
recently dead, had not long before been translated
from mere monarch to Empress. In Liverpool,
especially, the promotion must have seemed right.
Red-ensigned merchant ships carried half of the whole
world's water-borne international trade and the most
potently famous ships of British mercantile power, the
liners of Cunard and the White Star, were operated
from grandiose head offices on the Liverpool waterfront. Liverpool was the gateway of the British
Empire.

So many and so large were the fleets of passenger
and cargo liners captained and crewed by Liverpudlians, swarmed over and serviced by tens of thousands
of other citizens, that the scale and intensity of
ocean-going and coastal traffic made Liverpool a city
port like none had ever been before. A local journalist
and politician said in the 1920s that the Pierhead,
where the Liver Building stands, was a 'threshold to
the ends of the earth'.[2] That was true and a reminder of
it were the huge, verdigrised cormorants atop the two
cupolas of the Liver Building, their wings outstretched
to the Atlantic winds.

Calling at Liverpool in 1770 during his tour of some of
the Northern counties, Arthur Young said little of the
city except that its glory was '... the docks for the
shipping, which are much superior to any mercantile
ones in Britain'.[3] Remarks with that content were
common then and continued to be so in the century
that followed. Liverpool's people became accustomed to
thinking of themselves as belonging to a city with a
place in the *world*. Horizons were seldom lower than

that. Never down to the region and unthinkably not to the South-West corner of Lancashire.

The shipowners, merchants and bankers who epitomised Liverpool wealth were global operators who regularly needed to turn their backs on Lancashire and look outward to the countries bordering the Atlantic, Pacific and the Indian Oceans. Liverpool's seafarers, who brought the world home with them at the end of a voyage and stayed but a short time before embarking upon another, were no less cosmopolitan. Writing lyrically, but none the less accurately, Dixon Scott said of the port in 1907 that it was

> ... the city's *raison d'être*, the chief orderer and distributor of her people's vocations; and in that way ... interweaves class with class, provides merchant, clerk, seamen, and dock-labourers with a common unifying interest.[4]

Eighteenth- and nineteenth-century visitors were naturally impressed by the volume and tempo of shipping movements and cargo handling, but what unfailingly overawed them was the engineering coup involved in impounding almost one-third of the breadth of the river to create a tideless waterway. The seven-mile line of the river wall on the Liverpool side of the Mersey which enclosed the docks once marked the limit of low tide. Herman Melville was a typical admirer. Arriving in Liverpool on his first seafaring voyage in 1839, Melville began with slighting remarks on New York's port facilities and then compared Liverpool's dock with the Great Wall of China and the Pyramids of the Pharoahs. And if this now sounds extravagant, it was a commonplace comparison of its time.

Fifty years later Ramsay Muir, the University's professor of modern history, was no less impressed:

For seven miles and a quarter, on the Lancashire side of
the river alone, the monumental granite, quarried from
the [Mersey Docks and Harbour] Board's own quarries
in Scotland, fronts the river in a vast sea wall as solid
and enduring as the Pyramids ... Nor is this all.
Immense ugly hoppers, with groanings and clankings,
are perpetually at labour scooping out the channels of
the estuary ... Huge warehouses of every type ... front
the docks, and giant-armed cranes and other appliances
make disembarkation swift and easy. To a traveller
with any imagination few spectacles present a more
entrancing interest than that of these busy docks,
crowded with the shipping of every nation, echoing to
every tongue that is spoken on the seas, their wharves
littered with strange commodities brought from all the
shores of the oceans. It is here, beside the docks, that
the citizen of Liverpool can best feel the opulent
romance of his city ...[5]

River activity sent many writers reaching for their
pens. Another American literary figure, Nathaniel
Hawthorne, was installed as the United States' Consul
in Liverpool in the 1840s. Living on the Birkenhead
side of the river, he wrote in his diary that the

... parlour window has given us a pretty good idea of the
nautical business of Liverpool; the constant objects
being the little black steamers, puffing unquietly along
... sometimes towing a long string of boats from
Runcorn or otherwhere up the river, laden with goods;
– and sometimes gallanting in or out a tall ship ... Now
and then, after a blow at sea, a vessel comes in with her
masts broken short off in the midst, and marks of
rough handling about the hull. Once a week comes a
Cunard steamer, with its red funnel pipe whitened by
the salt spray; and firing off some cannon to announce
her arrival, she moors to a large iron buoy in the
middle of the river ... Immediately comes puffing
towards her a little mail-steamer, to take away her
mail-bags, and such of the passengers as choose to
land; and for several hours afterwards, the Cunarder
lies with the smoke and steam coming out of her, as if

she were smoking her pipe after some toilsome passage across the Atlantic.[6]

Thirty years later the Revd Francis Kilvert, much better known now than then, wrote in his diary that he had been to Liverpool's Exchange:

> ... one of the finest buildings of the kind in the world, and passing upstairs into the gallery and leaning upon the broad marble ledge we looked down upon a crowd of merchants and brokers swarming and humming like a hive of bees on the floor of the vast area below. All around the enormous hall were desks or screens or easels or huge slates covered with the latest telegrams, notices of London stock and share lists, cargoes, freights, sales, outward and homeward bound ships, times of sailing, state of wind and weather, barometer readings.[7]

The next day Kilvert took to the river:

> The Mersey was gay and almost crowded with vessels of all sorts moving up and down the river, ships, barques, brigs, brigantines, schooners, cutters, colliers, tugs, steamboats, lighters, 'flats', everything from the huge emigrant liner steamship with four masts to the tiny sailing and rowing boats. From the river one sees to advantage the miles of dock which line the Mersey side, and the forests of masts which crowd the quays ...[8]

Another clergyman, arriving in Liverpool from New York in the 1870s and writing for a New York newspaper, thought the city could be: '... aptly termed the "Chicago of England" [being] without doubt, essentially modern, and its rise and progress is something wonderful'.[9] In the docks the Revd Bell found a:

... long vista of vessels alongside the quay, lashed together with planks, reaching far ahead. There multitudes of goods are shipped – all kinds of hardware, railway supplies, iron in all shapes, of all kinds and sizes, sheet, wire, bar, spring, etc.; bales, boxes, casks, wines, spirits, ales, for India, Madagascar, Asia, Persia, the Continent and America ... Thousands of men are here measuring packages, invoicing goods, shipping merchandise; the tramp of horses, songs of stevedores, and shouts of sailors make a very Babel of industry.[10]

Major additions to the dock system appeared always as extensions of Liverpool's grandeur, as opportunities to reassert the role of the city as a world-scale port and trading centre. When the new Gladstone Dock was opened in 1927, F.C. Bowering, Lord Mayor, shipowner and a major force in world-wide marine insurance, reminded readers that Liverpool was still the pre-eminent liner port of the world and thought it appropriate also to remind the 'rest of the world' that:

... Liverpool was called into being, not as a terminus for ocean tourist traffic, but as a junction for the landing, embarkation and storage of the vast wealth exchanged between the North and Midlands of England and the overseas world.[11]

No exaggeration was involved when another writer in the special supplement of the local daily newspaper said: 'World-wide interest is aroused by the completion and opening of the greatest dock which the world has ever known ...'

The world role or claims to size measured on a global scale were a recurring feature of articles written about one or another of Liverpool's firms in the local press which was not then, nor subsequently, parochial. The *Journal of Commerce* was the more important of the

two national daily shipping papers and far superior to
the London-published *Lloyd's List*. The *Liverpool
Daily Post* was one of Britain's great Liberal
newspapers, if obviously inferior to the *Manchester
Guardian*.

The constant juxtaposition of Liverpool and the
world was not made extravagantly. It was presented
quietly and confidently. W.C. Stapledon, Chairman of
the Liverpool Steamship Owners' Association, running
through a list of the commodities imported through
Liverpool ends by saying: 'Almost all the world pours
in its tribute.'[13] Another shipowner points out that the
frequency of sailings from Liverpool to Calcutta is 'not
excelled in any other long-distance trade in the world'.[14]
An advertisement for the Cotton Exchange accurately
presents it as simply 'THE WORLD'S GREATEST
COTTON MARKET'.[15] In like vein the Stanley Dock
tobacco warehouse is 'the largest and most up-to-date
in the world'; the Liverpool Grain Storage and Transit
Company is 'one of the leading grain handling concerns
of the world'.[16] Waring and Gillows, meanwhile, have
so 'exquisitely furnished and equipped' Liverpool's
passenger liners that the city's fame 'as a centre for the
manufacture of the highest class of furniture has
spread all over the civilised world'.[17] The city's
merchants have also been busy, tapping

> huge consignments of cotton, corn, raw sugar,
> provisions, oil-bearing seeds, timber, fruit from over
> the seven seas of the world to the port of Liverpool.[18]

These cargoes and the ships carrying them were
insured in Liverpool, making it 'one of the world's
greatest insurance centres'.[19] Surveying all these
activities, the general manager of the Bank of
Liverpool and Martins, in 1927 the only remaining

major English bank with its head office outside London, said:

> It is fitting that reference should be made to a characteristic of Liverpool which impresses a new-comer. Expressed briefly, the cosmopolitan outlook and world-wide interests which exist make it the least parochial of our cities, and Liverpool may well be proud of her commanding position.[20]

Novelists, poets and autobiographers writing of their Liverpool connections place port, river, ships, merchants, shipowners and seafarers so firmly in the foreground that other activity appears secondary or absent altogether. As if to prove a once popular contention that Lime Street led to all parts of the Empire, there stands over the main entrance of Lewis's department store a large bronze figure by Sir Jacob Epstein: poised like Ulysses on a ship's prow, a muscular nude looks purposefully outward in the direction of the Western Approaches.

John Brophy's novel *City of Departures* is set in Liverpool at the end of the Second World War. His protagonist Charles Thorneycroft is returning to the city after artistic success in the metropolis and reflecting that if he had stayed in his native city he would have become '... a "local painter", deriving most of his income from formal portraits of aldermen and shipowners and cotton-brokers'.[21] Describing his city, Thorneycroft recalls that there was hardly ever a day without wind and that that, too, spoke of the sea and the port:

> The city air was fresh, it blew perpetually, strong or mild, off the sea and the river, and channelled its gusty way through every street. It ought to be a healthy air, and it had the tang of health, the odour of tidal salt

water, edged with smells from mud flats and sandhills
and shores strewn with seaweed. But it was not
healthy. It was laden with smoke and soot and grease,
and with smells from tanneries, breweries, oil-cake
factories, margarine factories, smells from the engine-
rooms of ships, from dockyards, from thousands of
warehouses where every sort of cargo was stored.[22]

Walking through the city streets noticing the grime
and dirt, the dinginess and the unrepaired bomb
damage, Charles Thorneycroft is depressed by the
contrast between what he sees and his boyhood
memories of a prideful, thriving place. But once on the
river he rediscovers Liverpool's urgency:

> Here where the ships sailed in and unloaded, loaded
> again and sailed out once more to all the oceans of the
> world, here was visible all around him a continuing
> magnificence. Here was no sign of lethargy or
> despondent regrets for the prosperities of the past.
> Here Liverpool was laying claim with a brawny fist to
> its own important place in the world.[23]

Helen Forrester's immensely popular three-volume
memoirs of growing up poor in Liverpool in the 1930s
are equally dependent upon the sea and ships for the
portrayal of possible employments and economic
activity. Helen Forrester's bankrupt father arrives
hoping to find work in a shipping company; outside the
Legs o' Man on Lime Street 'a number of seamen stood
laughing and joking';[24] an elderly gentleman on a park
bench 'interprets for Arab and Chinese seamen';[25] most
of the men on the dole had had jobs which 'were
dependent upon the ships which went in and out of
Liverpool in normal times';[26] near the Pierhead was 'an
arcade of tiny shops and offices where out-of-work
sailors lounged and spat tobacco'.[27]
Far more contemporary, saturated with recent

memory, is Matt Simpson's anthology of poems relating the benchmarks of childhood and adolescence in a waterfront district.[28]

Leaving the city to go to college, Matt Simpson says he was:

> ... the sailor's son who never put to sea.
> I left the city like
> the Cunard liners and returned
> to find their red and black
> familiar funnels gone from gaps
> between the houses where I'd lived,
> those girls become as vulgar as
> tattoos along my father's arms.[29]

And he recalls the streets of childhood:

> Salt winds keep these ocean-minded streets
> voyaging. There are men here who, landlubbered
> (wedded, winded, ulcered out), still walk as if
> steel decks were rolling underfoot; riggers
> and donkeymen, dockhands and chandlers,
> shipwrights and scalers, who service ships
> with something of love's habits, insisting on
> manhood and sweet memories.

> Look in one bedroom. On
> the glass-topped dressing table stood
> a carved war-painted coconut Aztec head –
> to me, memento mori, shrunken thing,
> who watched death dredge this bed.
> And yet for years it was a trophy,
> souvenir of all the thousand miles
> of furrowed brine, of fragrant isles.[30]

Cheek by jowl with the Liverpool of heroic feats of dock engineering, world-scale organisations of commerce and finance, and the sights and sounds of ships and cargoes there were less reputable institutions. As much a part of Liverpool as the respectability of business and other productive employments was the sailors' Liverpool, discreetly evoked here by a young ship's doctor in 1911:

> The sailor is the real king of Liverpool. Everybody in Liverpool loves the sailor, and is only too anxious to show him how to have a good time and spend his money while he is ashore; and it is he is the great man there till he has spent it.[31]

The young Dr Abraham, about to embark on his first voyage, was carefully echoing a rowdier rhetoric of the second half of the nineteenth century – that merchant seamen were essentially innocent, noble savages, preyed upon by a vicious class of semi-criminals ashore. So apparently effective were these beliefs that in Liverpool, as in other ports around the world, Sailors' Homes were being built from the 1830s onwards to provide sinless shelter. The oratory that might be employed to finance the construction of these Homes could not often have been more eloquent than that of the Revd Hugh McNeile at an inaugural meeting in Liverpool in 1844:

> If every sea is whitened with our canvas – every foreign harbour crowded with our ships – if from every country, and from every clime, there flows into our native land a full tide of all that ministers to the comforts, the conveniences, and the embellishments of life, to the materials of our productive industry, and the sinews of our national strength – it is to the energy and enterprise of our seamen that we are indebted for these blessings ... And what is the return we have made? What is the social and moral condition of that class to who we acknowledge these obligations? ... They

return, indeed, from distant scenes and barbarous
climes to the bosom of their countrymen, but they
return to be plundered and pillaged, seduced and
betrayed, by sharks and harpies ... they are so helpless
and so confiding ... they have had so little of the habit
or the means of becoming provident, that they
dissipate their hard-earned wages in a few days, and
are obliged to engage in any service, or embark on any
voyage, by which they may extricate themselves ...[32]

Charles Dickens was visiting Liverpool at this time
'keeping watch on Poor Mercantile Jack' and, as if not
to be outdone by the Revd McNeile, records a seaman

... with his hair blown all manner of wild ways, rather
crazedly taking leave of his plunderers. All the rigging
in the docks was shrill in the wind, and every little
steamer coming and going across the Mersey was sharp
in its blowing off, and every buoy in the river bobbed
spitefully up and down, as if there were a general
taunting chorus of 'Come along, Poor Mercantile Jack!
Ill-lodged, ill-fed, ill-used, hocussed, entrapped, anticipated, cleaned out. Come along, Poor Mercantile Jack,
and be tempest-tossed till you are drowned!'[33]

Dickens had visited Liverpool, he says, to join the
police for a night and to be shown 'the various unlawful
traps which are set every night for Jack'. Melville also
found ample provocation to moral outrage:

... of all seaports in the world, Liverpool, perhaps, most
abounds in all the variety of land-sharks, land-rats,
and other vermin, which make the hapless mariner
their prey. In the shape of landlords, bar-keepers,
clothiers, crimps, and boarding-house loungers, the
land-sharks devour him, limb by limb ...[34]

Although the Sailors' Home was soon built, the
intention of undermining the *dis*reputable part of
Liverpool's economy was never realised. Three decades

later, in 1879, the *Liberal Review* was saying that it
was an everyday thing '... to find seamen, the day after
their arrival in port, lying about the streets ... almost
naked, and in a stupefied state.'[35] And a full century
after Dickens, McNeile and Melville wrote so vividly of
the traps set for seafarers, a government publication in
the Second World War was using remarkably similar
language:

> In most port areas ... especially by the dockside, there
> are cafes and public houses of low type which can only
> be regarded as traps for the unwary seafarer. In these
> he may meet women of undesirable character, and may
> be induced to spend part of his wages in drink and
> entertainment of a harmful character.[36]

In post-war Liverpool the same 'traps' were still
there. The Duck House (because you had to duck your
head to get in through the low doorway) disappeared
with the old St John's market, right in the city centre,
in the 1960s. With it went the Eurasia, a Chinese
restaurant that brought together unattached seamen
and prostitutes without customers after the pubs
closed at ten-thirty in the evening. Mabel's down on
the dock road is still there, but now with a different
sort of customer; the same goes for the New Court Bar
on Victoria Street. One of the very last 'traps' still
going – if tottering – was in Upper Parliament Street,
described here by John Cornelius:

> The Lucky Bar was open all night, every night.
> Depending upon which ships were in dock, it could just
> as easily be chock-full on, say, a Tuesday night as on a
> Saturday. The 'business-girls', as they called them-
> selves, advised me to do as they did when trying to
> predict whether the club would be financially worth a
> visit or not: get a hold of a copy of *Lloyd's List* ... which
> gave details of which ships were due in the Port of

Liverpool. Ships could, of course, dock at any time of
day or night. Frequently, the Lucky would be almost
entirely devoid of male company, the girls sitting
quietly around the place, waiting. But at any time the
doorbell might ring and in would pour a gang of freshly
docked 'mushers' (seamen) ready for anything, wallets
bulging, banknotes flying like confetti.[37]

Melville would have understood the continuity, for,
while he could be frightening in the language of his
disapproval, he also knew that seamen were not quite
so innocent. Regretfully, he recorded:

> ... sailors love this Liverpool; and upon long voyages to
> distant parts of the globe will be continually dilating
> upon its charms and attractions, and extolling it above
> all other seaports in the world. For in Liverpool they
> find their Paradise – not the well known street of that
> name – and one of them told me he would be content to
> lie in Prince's Dock till he *hove up anchor* for the world
> to come.[38]

Liverpool necessarily had a very large transient
population comprised of visiting seafarers and those
who, at least notionally, were domiciled in the city. In
1872 the Chief Constable estimated that at any one
time, the city had a shifting population of about
20,000.[39] Although this figure is certainly inflated, the
social life of the sailor ashore was not lived in some
discreetly hidden and therefore ignorable quarter. The
most notorious cluster of streets by the turn of the
century were those in the vicinity of the Sailors'
Home(!), the Shipping Office where crews were
engaged and paid off, and the Seamen's Dispensary
which specialised in treating some of the better known
maladies. These streets were part of the heart of the
city, less than a five-minute walk from the colonnaded
entrance to the Liverpool branch of the Bank of

England and other financial emporia. The port had two public presences and, if the one was celebrated as much as the other was deplored, each was equally expressive of how the sea and its commerce possessed the city.

Ships, docks, cargoes and the people associated with them were, at the beginning of the twentieth century, Liverpool's past *and* future. In the twentieth century the city's economy did diversify into manufacturing, but it came late, was never sufficient and was too impermanent to offset the dramatic and headlong decline of the port from the late 1960s. The condition of Liverpool today – economically, politically, socially – is a direct outcome of the changing fortunes of the port.

In the 1890s the one-sidedness of Liverpool's economy had become a regular source of comment. The *Liverpool Review* remarked:

> We are not great as a manufacturing centre. By the side of Manchester, Leeds, Birmingham, Bradford and many smaller places we have as manufacturers to hide our heads.[40]

Comment had plainly become anxiety in the mid-Edwardian years when one of the local evening newspapers, the *Liverpool Express*, ran a competition for schemes to diversify the local economy. 'By 1914', says Francis Hyde referring to the port, 'the high peak of achievement had been reached and passed; the lean years were quickly recognised at the time.'[41] In 1923 a group of local businessmen co-operated with the relevant city and borough governments to found the first local promotional body:

> The Liverpool Organisation ... is influencing what people think about Liverpool the whole world over. It is broadcasting in every language its advantages as an

industrial centre and as a great seaport. It is in touch
with those who, abroad and at home, contemplate
setting up factories in this country. It acts as a clearing
house for information about the city, and ... it seeks,
persistently, to further the interests of the people of
Merseyside.⁴²

The language of intent and ambition in this ringing
declaration hardly varied at all in the subsequent
half-century as successor organisations set themselves
identical objectives.

Before 1914 the Port of Liverpool accounted for 31
per cent of the UK's visible imports and exports. By
1938 the Liverpool share had fallen to 21 per cent as
measured in value. The port's fortunes had for long
been linked to the cotton industry, and as Lancashire
textile manufacture declined, so too did Liverpool's
port. Britain's industrial centre was shifting to the
Midlands and other ports were within easier reach.

After the Second World War and with the post-war
boom in full swing the port did regain some of its lost
export trade. In the mid-1960s the dock road was in a
daily confusion of traffic; quays and dockside sheds
overpowered by haphazard queues of crated and
bundled and baled outward cargo. The regions of the
world were still sea-laned to Liverpool. Almost within
hailing distance of the Liver Building were small, low
ships running to Paris via Rouen, and a mere
ten-minute walk took in ships of varying sizes loading
for Limerick, Barcelona, New Orleans, Demerara,
Lagos and Manaos. Ford's had opened at Halewood and
sucked in hundreds of ex-seafarers, but it was still
impossible to exaggerate how much the city of
Liverpool was a seaport.

The main Post Office, next door to the Fruit
Exchange, could offer its customers the scents of fresh
Spanish oranges – or onions in another season. The

produce had come in to the city, via the North Queen's Dock, carried by the white-hulled ships of the MacAndrew's Line whose faded and peeling offering of 'fast cargo services to Spain' remains on the gable-end of a transit shed. Berthed nearby, then, were the Booth Line ships which traded first to Portugal and then to Brazil and as far up the Amazon as Manaos. An illicit trade in green parrots was a sideline for crew members.

A swing-bridge away from the Booth boats and tied up in Toxteth Dock were Elder Dempster Line ships. These were known throughout the port as the 'monkey boats' because where other ships kept cats these had once kept monkeys. The monkeys became part of the folklore of the city's South End and kept Elder Dempster's nickname going for they had done their bit in the Second World War. Late in the war, Captain Laurie James, then a young second officer, was in a convoy proceeding northward up the Portuguese coast and about to be attacked from the air:

> Now we had a monkey on this ship and they were the finest spotters of planes going. They had a very acute hearing; we called them grass monkeys and they were very small. They were the pets generally of somebody on board and they'd be looking in the direction of the 'plane and you could see them getting excited. It seemed as if they felt there was something menacing. This was well known amongst those of us on the West Coast trade.[43]

Elder Dempster's carried West African crews and had done so since before the First World War. Over the decades numbers of black seafarers had settled and married in Liverpool. They and their descendants provided a ready market for the yams, plantains and sweet potatoes sold to Granby Street shopkeepers by enterprising African seamen. African grey parrots, highly prized for their linguistic skills, also came off ships in the 'West Coast' trade. Some fetched prices still discussed in the bar-room talk of retired seafarers. Others ended up with Gran in the back kitchen, like the one remembered here by Matt Simpson:

> My father's brother brought it home,
> madcap Cliff, a 'case', with wit as wild
> as erotic dreams. It was his proof
> of Africa and emblem of the family pride
> in seamanship.[44]

The port also left its mark, if more obscurely, through its folk rituals. In the Protestant streets of the Dingle, at the southern-most end of the dock system, children ran through the streets at dawn on Good Friday dragging burning effigies of Judas Iscariot. As unknown in other parts of Liverpool as elsewhere in the UK, this was a Portuguese practice and seems to have arrived with the fruit trade. The Chinese New Year was an event in Liverpool before the rest of Europe had heard of it.

For the entire length of the dock road, the pubs either bore the names of the adjacent docks – the Coburg, the Bramley-Moore – or appealed to the ships, hence the Baltic Fleet and A1 at Lloyd's. Lime Street, no less than Le Canabière in Marseilles, had its American Bar and was similarly decorated with ships' photographs and mementoes deposited by sentimental departing seamen.

The businesses lining waterfront streets also announced their dependent livelihoods: makers of flags and bunting; chandlers specialising in deck and engineroom stores; bleaching agents and holystones for ships' wooden decks; Lion Brand patent packings

for steam valves and bales of colour-flecked, grey
cotton waste to clean engineroom ladders and plates.
Firms making paint, firms selling other people's.
Spinnaker Yacht Varnish: well spoken of by foremen
painters in Solent yachtyards and made in Liverpool to
withstand the weather thrown at the woodwork of
ocean liners. Tarpaulin and sailmakers. Ships did not
forsake canvas when they got rid of their sails. Around
the most modern motor ships there was canvas
everywhere. Canvas awnings to shade decks in the
tropics, covers for the deck lockers containing the
awnings. Tents for open hatches and at least three
tarpaulins to cover the forward hatches when at sea. If
the fancy canvas for gangway screens was made by the
ABs (able seamen), the rest of it was cut, shaped and
sewn ashore in the lofts which had once supplied
sailing ships.

The irregular roof line of the landward side of the
dock wall peaked with the grain and sugar silos, the
warehouses in grey-trimmed red brick, the unde-
corated castles of commerce giving shelter to bales of
wood and cotton. The city itself broke through the
workaday buildings, stood over the regiments and
battalions shifting cargoes, driving lorries, caulking
decks – and calculated their wages. At the Pierhead
the city intrudes into the docks and divides them into
North and South. Here are the grand buildings of
Edwardian opulence, fronting for the wealth once
made in owning and insuring ships; in lending money
to the merchants who bought and then sold unseen the
raw materials carried on homeward passages. Here in
Liverpool's City there were other and better dressed
regiments at work. Bowler hats and rolled umbrellas
were as *de rigueur* in Water Street as in London's
Leadenhall Street. On the morning and evening ferries
across the Mersey the bowler-hatted, and those

aspiring to the same rank, promenaded, anti-clockwise
and four abreast, around the boatdecks. The old
custom was defiantly maintained in the late 1960s
although the ranks had thinned compared with the
phalanxes once common. The business side of ship
operation and other shipping services, not to mention
banking and insurance, were all labour-intensive
activities. Literally thousands of office workers poured
into the city every day. Clerks and typists from the
inner suburbs of Liverpool and Wallasey; managers
and directors from West Kirby and Blundell Sands.

Moving ships, cargoes and money from one part of
the world to another by telex and cable was, on its own,
a fair-sized economy with its own ring of satellite
firms. Every large firm had its organisational formula
and accordingly provided work for the local printshops
and bookbinders. Ships' chart folios went ashore to
chart correctors' offices for the latest marine hazards to
be entered in indian ink; ships' chronometers and
barographs were landed to be cleaned and rated. Men
from Sperry, Marconi and Decca went down to ships to
check gyro compasses, radios and radars respectively.
Board of Trade surveyors checked ships' safety
equipment while their examiner colleagues tested and
grilled the young mates and engineers temporarily
ashore studying for their certificates of competency.

In other offices scattered around the city were the
average adjusters to settle claims between the insured
and the insurer; the ship-brokers to buy, sell or charter
a ship; the freight forwarders to arrange shipment of
crates or bales of anything to anywhere; the agencies
to handle the business of foreign ships; the foreign
consular corps to guide and advise resident and
visiting nationals. The Dock Board in its magnificent
offices of marble and mahogany had its own army of
clerks, managers and superintendants to watch over

and log in and out its revenue and expenses, its pier-masters and dockgatemen, the crews of buoyage ships, dredgers and floating cranes; the gangs of skilled tradesmen and their labourers who ran the internal railway system, the water hydraulic lines and pump-houses which angled cranes and swung bridges; the shipwrights, millwrights, boilermakers, ironmoulders and blacksmiths who made and maintained the lock-gates and their machinery.

A ship arriving in daylight would be certain to find on the quayside waiting groups of men whose purposes were in their clothes and in their manner. A dark-suited and homburged Marine Super come to welcome home his charge and wanting a briefing of immediate ship's requirements from the master. The master stevedore to see the Mate about readiness to discharge cargo and to say what he wants first out of the holds. The riggers waiting to clatter their boots up the gangway, to open up hatches and top derricks. Customs rummagers to look for contraband. The Port Health wanting reassurance on the absence of infectious diseases. The union reps come to collect dues, pin down evasive members and hoping to avoid complaints. A tailors' runner, briefcase bursting with samples of suitings, swift with the tape and the sizes into dog-eared notebook, talking con-stantly of other ships just in and how he saw old so-and-so only yesterday. More sheepishly, a mate newly gone ashore tours the officers' accommodation hopeful of selling some life insurance. With *bonhomie* a padre or two from the Church of England Mission to Seamen and the Roman Catholic Apostleship of the Sea come looking for the faithful, the sad and lonely, leaving calling cards and posters advertising their service. Less welcome by far, the evangelical tract pedlars for whom seafarers might imaginatively ham up their sinfulness.

On the first night ashore the port's evening economy

provided voluntary as well as revenue-generating
services. Of the former, and hugely popular with
seamen, were the dances run by the Apostleship of the
Sea at Atlantic House. Parish organisations were then
still strong, parishioners still obedient and young
women kept close to the church. It was almost
sufficient for the word to go out from Atlantic House to
the parishes and dozens of women would arrive to do
their Christian duty and dance with the seamen.

When the whaling fleet docked in Liverpool
overnight to discharge its cargoes of Antarctic oils,
women distinctly without the imprimatur of the
priesthood were in town and in number. On those
nights Lime Street could seem like a Hollywood set of
San Francisco in the days of the gold rush. The men
came up town from the Gladstone Dock with a lot of
money and a determination to obliterate the six
months in the frozen wilds of South Georgia. The big
money and the number of men drew women in from St
Helens and Wigan and Salford.

Of the other Liverpool that had little to do with ships
except through family and history, a substantial part
either lived off processing cargoes or worked for firms
needing the volume generated by ships to cover their
basic costs. Ships arriving from a foreign voyage
brought with them a hidden cargo of dirtied bed linen
and towels which sustained a number of laundries. It
was not coincidence either that Britain's largest
dry-cleaning firm, Johnson's, was close to the local
waterfront: it had a handsome business in cleaning the
curtains and loose covers from the public rooms of the
passenger and cargo liners. Bits and pieces of
port-related employment of this sort contributed many
hundreds of jobs to the local economy – but not nearly
as many as the big processing industries.

At its peak, the port provided direct employment for perhaps as many as 60,000 people. Almost as many again worked in the processing and manufacturing industries that were only in Liverpool or its close hinterland through a dependence on the port's commodities. When Bryant and May built their model match factory close to Garston Docks just before the Second World War, they could draw upon the standards of Baltic timber brought in on lop-sided ships. It made sense, too, for BICC to build its insulated cable factories on Liverpool's borders: ships of the Blue Funnel brought in latex from Malaya and Sumatra and those of Pacific Steam carried copper from Chile. Lever Brothers at Port Sunlight took copra off the Bank Line ships which had ferried it home from the Pacific Islands and palm oil from Nigeria off ships of their own fleet ... and then gave it back again in bars of soap to be distributed around Scotland and the North-East of England by the Coast Line's weekly sailings to Aberdeen and Newcastle.

The British American Tobacco Company made cigarettes and Ogden's pipe tobacco from leaf brought in by the Harrison boats from South and East Africa and the USA. And so the connections went. The mills of Rank and Spiller and Wilson ground the grains of Canada and the US mid-West as Joseph Heap's mill husked the rice of India and Burma. The Crawford family's factories mixed, so to speak, Rank's flour with Tate and Lyle's sugar to bake their biscuits. Meanwhile and nearby, other factories – Read's and Tillotson's – made tins and cartons for the biscuits and the cigarettes. Courtauld's first rayon plant – then British Enka – overlooked the Grand National course in the suburb of Aintree and fed itself on imported Canadian woodpulp. Evans Medical, now absorbed into the pharmaceutical giant Glaxo, began life in

docklands producing tinctures, powders and pills from
exotic spices, roots, herbs and seeds. Before finally
leaving Liverpool, Tate and Lyle had absorbed all its
other cane sugar refining competitors in the city to
become the largest refinery in the world.

A manufacturing sector independent of the port did
develop in the inter-war years. 'The Automatic', now
part of Plesseys, produced telephone exchange equipment, employed 16,000 at its peak and was just about
the only representative in Liverpool of the growing
consumer durable industry of the 1930s. Elsewhere in
the city during the 1930s, rearmament saw huge new
factories making air frames, vehicles and aero engines.
These were the very first factories to be directed by
central government to Liverpool and represented
recognition by the state of Liverpool's need for a
broader based economy.

The armament factories were sold off early in the
peace after 1945 to become satellite factories for
English Electric, GEC, Lucas and Dunlop. Ironically,
these were among the first to be caught in the big wave
of factory closures in Britain in the late 1960s and
which continued through the 1970s and 1980s. It was
unfortunate for Liverpool's working people that the
desperate attempts by senior British managements to
overcome their archaism and incompetence which had
produced the flood of factory closures, should have
come at a time when the port was suffering from the
final expiry of the imperial connection, entry into the
EEC and containerisation of non-bulk sea-borne
commerce.

Since the 1920s there had been an underlying shift
of the axis of UK manufacturing industry from North
to South-East and so attempts to attract factory-based
employments had always gone against the national
trend. The *Liverpool Daily Post* reported in 1954 that
although nearly 60 non-Merseyside firms (including

Dunlop, GEC and others) had opened factories and created jobs for 27,000 people, this had not been sufficient to alter the economy of the area radically.[45] Five years later Mr John Rodgers, MP, Parliamentary Secretary to the Board of Trade, said that no area of similar size anywhere in the UK had employment problems remotely comparable. He went on to say that although there were new factories being built, progress was still not good enough.[46] The outlook had not improved in 1962 when the North West Regional Board for Industry said: 'The amalgamation and rationalisation of firms on Merseyside was resulting in a loss of employment opportunities in an area where unemployment was a serious problem.'[47] The car industry, then arriving, was to provide only temporary relief. The port and its related processing industries therefore continued to provide the city's core. Although the number of jobs in this core steadily shrank during the 1950s and 1960s, it could still appear to be the one area of economic activity that was deeply rooted.

Until the mid-1960s the Port of Liverpool's share in the national totals of imports and exports had remained more or less constant. Liverpool's prominence came from cargo liners and these, of course, were precisely the type of ship that were soon to be replaced by the container ships. The table overleaf, showing the arrivals of large container ships in 1985, starkly illustrates Liverpool's decline as a port.

The movements of manufacturing industry, population and wealth to the South-East inevitably made the region's ports more attractive to shippers of goods. The coastal ports of the South-East, being tidal, were also much cheaper to use than Liverpool's enclosed dock systems which were expensive to maintain. At the same time the decline of Commonwealth countries as trading partners and the rise of EEC countries obviously left Liverpool marooned on

Arrivals at Selected UK Ports of Large Container Ships, 1985

Port of arrival	Number of container vessels of more than 20,000 tonnes
London	156
Southampton	272
Liverpool	76
Clyde	54
Felixstowe	496

Source: Department of Transport, *Port Statistics*, 1986

the wrong side of the country. Between 1966 and 1985 Liverpool's share of all ship arrivals in the UK was halved while Dover's share increased four-and-a-half times. By 1985 the East coast ports had totally eclipsed the importance of those to the West. The following 'league table' of UK ports in 1966 and 1985 provides a neat illustration of the transformation of Britain's patterns of sea-borne trade.

Between 1966 and 1985 the relative importance of East and West coast ports was reversed. In 1966 there were only four East coast ports in the top ten whereas in 1985 there were only four West coast ports. Dover and Felixstowe which *together* handled one-ninth of the volume of Liverpool's goods in 1966 were both, *separately*, handling 10 per cent more than Liverpool in 1985. Containerisation went in parallel with the shift of traffic to the East Coast, although the timing of the two movements was largely a coincidence. The impact on port and shipping operations of the containerisation of cargoes was swifter and greater

Ten Largest UK Ports, 1966 and 1985*

1966	1985
1 London	1 London
2 Liverpool	2 Tees and Hartlepool
3 Tees and Hartlepool	3 Grimsby and Immingham
4 Manchester	4 Felixstowe
5 Clyde	5 Dover
6 Hull	6 Liverpool
7 Newport (Mon.)	7 Clyde
8 Bristol	8 Medway
9 Port Talbot	9 Port Talbot
10 Grimsby and Immingham	10 Manchester

Source: National Ports Council (1967) and Department of Transport (1985)

* As measured by volume of foreign and domestic non-oil traffic for 1985 and non-fuel traffic for 1966.

than the transition from sail to steam. Until the 1960s ships carrying frozen or manufactured goods were loaded in much the same way as furniture removal vans – giving due consideration to stability, items were packed in accordance to shape and with a view to minimising lost space. In 1927 it was reckoned not surprising to see in the list of cargo of a ship loading for the Far East:

> ... a ton or two of bicycles, a ton of metal polish, three tons of sewing thread, two of boracic acid, nearly a ton of blotting paper, ten tons of biscuits, a hundred of soap, twenty of whiskey or stout, and as much as four tons of assorted chocolates.[48]

If the list was perhaps slightly different by the 1960s, a comparable variety was nevertheless packed into the same space. Even homogeneous cargoes like cane sugar were still coming into the port in bags until the early 1950s – and the description which follows of moving from bagged to bulk sugar stands as a useful analogy for the transition from handling individual goods to stowing containers:

> The first bulk cargo of raw sugar was received in Liverpool, in the S.S. *Sugar Transporter*, in August 1952, and, once bulk receiving started, the amount in bags gradually decreased to vanishing point, taking with it the old-fashioned method of weighing at the docks, the trailer wagons that carried the bags to the refinery and the gangs whose job it was to open and empty the bags in the silo bays, which now stand generally idle. Gone, too, was the livelihood of the man who made sack hooks ...[49]

The containerisation of general cargoes was first successfully introduced in the 1950s on the West coast of the USA where it showed spectacular savings in the time ships spent in port. One US study showed that where it took 10,584 working hours to load and unload 11,000 tons of general cargo it took only 546 working hours to load and unload 11,000 tons of containers.[50]

The capital cost of containerising general and frozen cargoes was simply enormous; special ships had to be built; quays and cargo-handling equipment reconstructed and replaced; stocks of the steel boxes built up; compensation paid to dock labourers whose considerable skills were being made redundant. This gave a premium to new port sites like Felixstowe where there were no costs involved in scrapping obsolescent equipment and no compensation to be paid to displaced workers.

The most visible consequence of containers, and the one the public knew about, was the large reduction in the number of dockers' jobs. Less visible because hardly publicised were the effects on seafarers and those who serviced ships. Container ship operation became almost identical to that of tankers which had for long been accustomed to port turn-around times of less than 24 hours. This mode of operation meant that most ship maintenance was done by ships' crews rather than by ship repair firms who had previously swarmed over ships during their lengthy stays in port. For their part seafarers were plainly affected by a type of ship that on the Australasian routes, for example, halved the voyage time once normal (from five months to two-and-a-half), could carry the equivalent of six traditional cargo liners and needed only half the crew of one of them. These ships, too, were now completely bare of their own cargo-handling gear, while a conventional six-hatch ship had had twenty derricks, each with its own set of winches. Here there were effects upon the rigging lofts and the rope manufacturers. Shipowners themselves, now operating fewer ships, no longer needed such large staffs ashore creating yet further employment consequences.

It took little more than a single decade for Liverpool's port to shrink so much that it became almost unrecognisable. Herman Melville and all those other celebrated nineteenth-century visitors would still have found something to recognise in the mid-1960s, for although ships might have changed, the cargoes they carried and the methods of handling them were sufficiently similar to have been recognisable. By the early 1980s most of the dock system had changed and been converted to other uses. The port that had created Liverpool had dwindled to insignificance and left the city with huge economic and political problems.

But the port had also bequeathed to Liverpool a special social character. And so in their ways of thinking, feeling and acting, the city's people remained lively, assertive and self-confident.

Notes

1 N. Pevsner, *The Buildings of England (South Lancashire)*, Harmondsworth 1968, p.148.
2 Michael O'Mahoney, *Liverpool Ways and Byeways*, Liverpool 1931, p.84.
3 Arthur Young, *A Six Months Tour Through The North of England*, Vol II, London 1771, p.167.
4 Dixon Scott, *Liverpool*, London 1907, pp.14-5.
5 Ramsay Muir, *A History of Liverpool*, London 1907, p.301.
6 Nathaniel Hawthorne, *The English Notebooks*, New York 1941, p.21.
7 William Plomer (ed.), *Kilvert's Diary, 1870-1879*, Harmondsworth 1982, p.193.
8 Ibid., p.193.
9 Revd Fred Bell, *Midnight Scenes in the Slums of New York*, New York n.d. (c.1880), p.210.
10 Ibid., p.230-1.
11 *Supplement to Liverpool Daily Post*, 19 July 1927, p.4.
12 Ibid., p.26.
13 *Supplement to Liverpool Daily Post*, 21 February 1927, p.19.
14 Ibid., p.25.
15 Ibid., p.58.
16 Ibid., p.45.
17 Ibid., p.31.
18 Ibid., p.57.
19 Ibid., p.55.
20 Ibid., p.53.
21 John Brophy, *City of Departures*, London 1946, p.12.
22 Ibid., p.36.
23 Ibid., p.42.
24 Helen Forrester, *Twopence to Cross the Mersey*, London 1985, p.13.
25 Ibid., p.125.
26 Ibid., p.74.
27 Ibid., p.87.
28 Matt Simpson, *Making Arrangements*, Newcastle-upon-Tyne, 1982.

29 Ibid., p.30.
30 Ibid., p.21.
31 J.J. Abraham, *The Surgeon's Log*, London 1911, p.6.
32 *Report of a Public Meeting of the Principal Shipowners, Merchants and Inhabitants of Liverpool*, Liverpool, 1844, pp.6-7.
33 Charles Dickens, 'Poor Mercantile Jack', Chapter 5, *The Uncommercial Traveller*, n.d. (Odhams edn), pp.39-40.
34 Herman Melville, *Redburn*, Harmondsworth, 1977, p.202.
35 *Liberal Review*, 30 August 1879.
36 Ministry of Labour and National Service, *Seamen's Welfare in Ports*, London 1943, p.20.
37 John Cornelius, *Liverpool 8*, London 1982, p.66.
38 Melville, op.cit., p.202.
39 *House of Commons Select Committee on Habitual Drunkeness*, 1872, para. 2140.
40 *Liverpool Review*, 26 July 1890.
41 F.E. Hyde, *Liverpool and The Mersey*, Newton Abbot 1971, p.141.
42 *Supplement to Liverpool Daily Post*, 21 February 1927, p.35.
43 Capt. L. James, retired master, Elder Dempster Lines, in an interview with the author, April 1986.
44 Simpson, op.cit., p.11.
45 *Liverpool Daily Post*, 23 February 1954.
46 Ibid., 14 January 1959.
47 Ibid., 27 March 1962.
48 *Supplement to Liverpool Daily Post*, 21 February 1927, p.22.
49 J.A. Watson, *A Hundred Years of Sugar Refining*, Liverpool 1973, pp.66-7.
50 P. Ross, 'Waterfront Labour Response to Technological Change', *Labour Law Journal*, 1970, p.399.

2 The Old Families

The 'old families' who in mid-nineteenth-century Liverpool came to be regarded as the local aristocracy were not obviously qualified for the label. Few had been resident for more than three generations and they were not always the most conspicuously rich. But the names did have a cachet and this was based upon evidence of recurring commitment to civic duty. Without flamboyant display they practiced *noblesse oblige* in the city in the same way that landowning families were supposed to practise it in the country-side. They sat on committees that offered no direct financial gain but which improved the quality of public life; their names were on the subscription lists raising money for good works and public projects. Newcomers making new fortunes and needing to establish their social importance added their names to the subscription lists and by the second generation became 'old families' too. But just as the regularly replenished stock of 'old family' names became most luminous, commercial developments were eroding the basis of individualised power and influence.

Where original fortunes had usually been made in three or four-handed partnerships, continuing expansion after the mid-nineteenth century increasingly meant bringing in outside capital which eventually undermined private control. By the first decade of the twentieth century partnerships and family firms were being absorbed into public companies with little or no attachment to Liverpool. The 'old families' left their names on streets, on docks, on university buildings, on bequests to art galleries and even left a few descendants to keep an eye on old endowments. By the 1950s none were left to wield significant economic or political power, although their influence has in other ways proved remarkably durable: the proud rhetoric they used to insist the stature of Liverpool as a world city sent down deep roots amongst all classes of the people.

Uncovering the lives of the rich and the powerful is not a simple matter. If the rich and their partners in the professional classes have always been able to commission investigations into the lives and circumstances of the poor and working classes, few have chronicled the lives of the rich. As we shall see in the next chapter, there is an abundance of information on the lives of Liverpool's dockland people, but the evidence for employers is fragmentary.

Investigations by W.D. Rubinstein have shown that, London apart, Liverpool produced more wealthy

families in the nineteenth century than any other
English city. At its peak, in the years 1880-1899,
Liverpool produced as many millionaires as Greater
Manchester, West Yorkshire, West Midlands,
Tyneside and East Anglia combined. Taking a longer
period, from 1804 to 1914, Merseyside produced almost
twice as many millionaires as Greater Manchester
and, outside London, was only surpassed by Clydeside.
At lower levels of wealth Liverpool remained equally
prominent. Taking Schedule D on tax on profits from
business and the professions as an indicator, in the
year 1879–80 Liverpool, with a population of 552,000
contributed £11 million, while Birmingham, Bristol,
Leeds and Sheffield with a combined population of
1,200,000 contributed slightly less, £10.8 million. Even
into the twentieth century Liverpool continued to
produce large fortunes. Between 1920 and 1969, only
Clydeside had as many estates valued at more than
£0.5 million.

London consistently generated greater wealth for

*Number of UK Estates Valued at More Than £500,000,
1920-1969, excluding London*

Region	Number of estates
Clydeside	64
Merseyside	64
West Yorks.	59
Greater Manchester	49
Greater Birmingham	47

Source: W.D. Rubinstein[1]

families than the rest of Britain. The fortunes were
made in banking, finance, insurance, shipping and
commodity-broking, not in cotton and woollen textiles,
in shipbuilding and engineering. Only in soft manufac-
tures – such as sugar refining, tobacco processing and
brewing and distilling – were large fortunes made in
the capital. In all these respects, Liverpool was a
mirror image of London.

Where shipowning was concerned, Liverpool was on
a par with London. London had the P&O which carried
the servants and soldiers of the Raj to India, but their
most opulent ships were excelled by those of the
Cunard, the White Star and other Liverpool companies
which monopolised the North Atlantic. The relative
strength and independence of Liverpool shipowners
was demonstrated by the Liverpool Steamship
Owners' Association which retained its independence
of the London-based organisation until the 1960s. In
the nineteenth century Liverpool was the major
provincial banking centre and Liverpool banks were
critical to many a Lancashire and West Riding textile
mill. The Liverpool-based Martins Bank was the last
big provincial bank to be merged into the 'big five' – it
was absorbed by Barclays in the 1960s. Liverpool was
also the most important centre for insurance outside
London, and Royal Insurance still has its head office in
Liverpool.

The best source on Liverpool's main firms in the late
nineteenth century is B.G. Orchard's *Liverpool's Legion
of Honour* in which 296 firms are singled out as being
the city's 'grandest'.[2] In this roll call there are 38
'shipowners and merchants', 41 'cotton-brokers', 47
'merchants'. A further 137 firms all provided services
of one kind or another. A mere 33 were manufacturers,
of which only a handful were major employers. In the
metal industries only five were listed – a copper

smelter, two ironfounders and two shipbuilders. These figures confirm the picture of the city's dependence on the port presented in the last chapter.

Until the First World War when most of the rich were still resident – in the region, if not in the city itself – the hierarchy of wealth was generally known and understood. The wealthiest and most prestigious were literally household names and they and their families' activities would be noted in their own circles and regularly reported on – where visible – in the local daily, weekly and periodical press. At this time the national press was still fairly new and the range and detail provided by local journalists was extensive. The predominance of the local press merely reflected the fact that social orientations were still largely local.

The major shipowners and merchants were invariably engaged in businesses that pulled their horizons far beyond Liverpool. Liverpool was a place from which they looked *outwards*. It was a base for their activity only in the sense that they had to have offices somewhere to centralise their operations. The local network of commerce and finance was convenient, but few, if any, of their strategic business considerations took solely local factors into account. Instructive here are the business histories of Cunard, Blue Funnel (Alfred Holt's) and Harrison's written by Francis Hyde.[3] In each of these accounts we find that as the businesses expanded through the second half of the nineteenth century, the more extensively were the companies drawn into organising a global operation. The MacIvers, who were running Cunard during the company's critical growth period, depended on government contacts in London and Washington to safeguard the subsidies paid through mail contracts. They also needed to nurture key agencies in the USA and Europe to sell berths in their ships. The Holts, for their part,

were organising agencies and trading companies in the
Far East to fill their ships with outward and
homeward cargoes.

Shipowners involved in foreign trade, including
those with relatively small fleets, could only survive in
the long term with reliable international connections.
Their perspectives followed their ships to their termini
and the very fact of operating across national
boundaries obliged them to work through contacts
with foreign governments and the officers of the
British consular and diplomatic corps. The ships
themselves might be registered, repaired, provisioned
and crewed in Liverpool, but that was a matter of
historical evolution of the company and of convenience.
It was not a matter of necessity. The outward
orientation of shipowners was also seen within the
influential communities of bankers, insurers and
commodity-brokers. When the Bank of England
appointed its local agent it was necessarily sensitive to
the need for someone familiar with international
trade. The Bank's Liverpool agent in 1892 was Thomas
Agnew who, apart from having had the good sense to
marry the granddaughter of a former Governor of the
Bank of England, had previously worked for a firm of
shipowners and underwriters as well as for merchant
houses specialising in trade with India, China and
South America.[4] For reasons that hardly need
elaborating, merchants had to be cosmopolitans. While
merchants of softwood timber looked westward to the
Atlantic and Pacific coasts of North America and
eastward to Russia and Scandinavia, hardwood
merchants looked to Central and Southern America, to
West Africa, Malaya and Burma. Cotton merchants
were most at home in New Orleans and Charleston,
but were also well connected in Alexandria and
Bombay. And as ships increased in capital value and

cargoes in size, marine insurers looked to sell on part of their risks in the USA and to insurers in Western European ports.

If the outwardness of the big battalions of Liverpool's wealth was given in the first instance by the very nature of the business, global reach grew more extensive with every increase in scale. This has already been suggested with brief references to Cunard and Alfred Holt's, and can be seen in more detail in another example, this time of Elder Dempster's. The firm bought land in West Africa to build workshops, offices, cold stores, hotels and slipways; through a subsidiary, it also owned West African mineral concessions, mines, quarries, sawmills, forests, factories, railways and tramways. In Liverpool the firm owned cartage and stevedoring companies as well as warehousing, and in South Wales owned collieries to provide coal for Elder Dempster ships. The production, distribution and sale of coal was itself a small-scale empire:

> Cheap and reliable sources of suitable coal were found at Garth and Maesteg in Glamorgan, and the collieries were bought. They were then operated by Elders Navigation Collieries Limited. Bunkers were subsequently supplied to Elder Dempster vessels, via Port Talbot, at the main UK ports and at Las Palmas, Tenerife and Freetown. Supplies at these latter places were in the hands of wholly-owned subsidiary firms ... and they not only provided fuel for Elder Dempster's own vessels but catered for a very wide market. Bunkers for the Admiralty, for many foreign navies and for over 200 different shipping lines meant the sale of a quarter of a million tons annually from Las Palmas.[5]

At the same time as Sir Alfred Jones was establishing this business empire in the Canaries, the Gambia, Sierra Leone, the Gold Coast, Nigeria and the Belgian

Congo in the name of Elder Dempster, the Holts and
their partners were creating a similar vertically
integrated group of companies and agencies in the Far
East. To get into the Dutch East Indies they created a
Dutch company and put ships under the Dutch flag,
established a subsidiary line linking Bangkok and
Singapore, bought out a competing company operating
from London, bought into and then took over a line
establishing links between Australia and Singapore.
All this in addition to a string of subsidiaries, jointly
owned with agency companies, which operated
wharfage, storage and lighterage concerns.[6] This
global business structure formed by the 1890s was
eminently rational. By integrating adjacent operations
the core shipowning activity was increasingly pro-
tected from uncertainty. But the extent of the overall
operation took the firm a long long way from its local
origins. The scale of organisation at mid-century had
been profoundly different and business practice itself
far less specialised. The Swires' activities, described
here by Sheila Marriner and F.E. Hyde, were typical:

> In the early 1850s, they received consignments from
> New York, New Orleans, Boston, Nova Scotia, Oporto,
> Antwerp, Havre, Rotterdam and Montreal. The
> products they handled included cheese, pork, wine,
> earthenware, lard, wool, hams, beer, glass, cigars,
> apples, flour, iron and steel wares, clothing and, most
> important of all, raw cotton. In addition, they owned
> some small shares in ships.[7]

Shipowning, merchanting, commodity-broking and
marine insurance, too, were commonly combined in the
mid-nineteenth century, although each activity was
soon to become a speciality despite the fact that the old
practice of dividing shares in ships into sixty-fourths
was still common as late as the 1890s. This system

frequently allowed such people as prosperous artisans, dealers, innkeepers and shopkeepers to dabble in shipowning, although the bigger ships and regular traders were share-owned through the friends, family and business circles of the merchant elite.

The practices of mixing merchanting with shipowning and insurance, together with the dividing of ownership of ships, created economic relations that were simultaneously social relations. These relations were then cemented through regular meetings on the trading floor of the Exchange, on committees of local charities and foundations, at church on Sundays, at events at the Wellington Assembly Rooms and through intermarriage.

Naturally, different sections of Liverpool's elite moved in their own circles of Liberal and Conservative organisations, of the Unitarian, Methodist, Baptist or Anglican congregations – but they would all meet again at the Steamship Owners' and other trade associations. Most, if not all, circles overlapped and the launching of one or another civic venture would quickly produce cross-sectional support. In 1880 William Rathbone was involved in raising funds for the new university college and gave the following oversimplified if essentially accurate account of how it was done:

As soon as the election was over in 1880, I went to my two brothers and asked them if they would join me in founding a Professorship. They ageed to do so. I then went to Alexander Brown [merchant], who had promised £5,000, and to William Crosfield [soap manufacturer], who was the first to promise £1,000, and suggested that if Crosfield would induce each of his partners to do the same, they and Brown could found a 'Gladstone Professorship' ... I then went to Mr Balfour and Mr Samuel Smith, as Scotchmen, and pointed out that, as the Scotch had been fifty years ahead of us in education, and with the good education they had, many of them came to Liverpool and realized large fortunes – it would be a graceful thing if the Scotch merchants of Liverpool would found a Professorship of Political Economy and Moral Philosophy. To this they agreed ... I then went to my corn-market friends, Mr Paul and Mr J. Brigham ... leading off with good donations ...[8]

Rathbone, a Liberal MP for a Liverpool seat, then goes on to say how he recruited two former Conservative Mayors of the city, Messrs Forwood and Royden, both shipowners, to fund another chair and how Lord Derby, major Liverpool landowner and resident just outside the city, was persuaded to fund a chair of natural history. Just a few years later, in 1885, William Rathbone once again acted as a 'broker' for the establishment of a department of engineering at the university: he recruited John Brunner (chemical manufacturer), Alfred Holt, Thomas Ismay and Thomas Harrison, (shipowners), and Sir Andrew Walker (brewer).[9]

Of those who accumulated substantial wealth, few seem to have been natives of Liverpool in the first generation, and in this respect Liverpool was similar to other port cities. M.J. Daunton has written of Cardiff that men moved there to engage in merchanting coal and operating ships, and 'Often they left once they had made their fortune. Usually they had no ties with the locality or town.'[10] This observation repeats contemporary complaints made of Liverpool. Speaking of Liverpool in the second half of the nineteenth century, Orchard says that some lucrative branches of trade – he mentions provisions, metals, and timbers – as well as a large colony of prosperous merchants from the European mainland

... have given us no family of real importance although

from them have sprung scores of clever, prosperous
traders, who worked for their thirty, forty, or fifty years
without manifesting one spark of patriotic or civic fire.
While with us they were not of us; their hearts (if they
had hearts) were elsewhere; and having accumulated
enough, they disappeared, most of them to reappear in
some more fashionable locality.[11]

Of specific social origins relatively little is known
except that there does not seem to be a proverbial 'rags
to riches' story. If some had little material capital from
their families on which to build, they nevertheless had
social and cultural capital provided by education and
the climate of outlook and ambition in family background. Thomas Ismay's background was probably
fairly typical even if his later career was not. Ismay
arrived in Liverpool from Maryport in 1853 to be
apprenticed, at the age of sixteen, to a firm of ship-
brokers who were his father's Liverpool agents. Ismay
had previously been educated at a then progressive
academy in Carlisle; his father, a timber merchant,
shipbuilder and shipbroker, was comfortably off. At the
age of thirty Ismay played the leading role in a
partnership which founded the White Star Line. Ten
years later he had bought an estate in the Wirral
overlooking the Dee estuary and the Clwyd hills.

Sir Alfred Jones, from less promising circumstances,
became just as wealthy while living far less
conspicuously. Born in Carmarthen and moving to
Liverpool as a child after his father had sold his
proprietorship of a local newspaper, Jones seems to
have been well educated. Leaving school at fourteen to
make one voyage to sea as a cabin boy, Jones then
began work as a junior clerk in a shipping agent's
office. His biographer has calculated that after Jones
reached his thirty-ninth birthday he added an average
of £22,000 per annum to his capital, i.e. without taking

into account the income consumed by living 'at a very comfortable level'.[12]

Other rich shipowners were celebrated neither in their lifetimes nor subsequently, and their origins, if discoverable, remain obscure. Sir Edward Bates made a large fortune in trade with India where he had lived for twenty years before arriving in Liverpool. Reckoned to come originally from Hull, long before his sixtieth birthday he had a castle in Wales, a town house in Liverpool, a country house and at least two landed estates.

Charles Booth, the famous investigator of London poverty in the 1890s, was third generation in Liverpool of a family who had originally been farmers near Warrington. Charles and his brother grew wealthy as merchants and shipowners. Through his marriage to a Mary Macaulay, Charles became related to the famous Victorian historian, Lord Macaulay, to Robert Holt, a Liverpool shipowner, and to Beatrice Webb, the most famous of the Fabians.[13] Within a few years Booth had moved to London and by 1886 the business had done well enough for him to buy Gracedieu Manor, in Leicestershire where '... social contacts were established with neighbouring landowners from which resulted joint "shoots" for the benefit of his sons and guests ...'[14]

The Holts originated in Halifax, the Rathbones in Rochdale, the MacIvers in the Scottish Lowlands, the Harrisons from Garstang near Preston. Through trading connections with Liverpool all the families mentioned here – as well as hundreds of others – had recognised in Liverpool a city of expanding opportunity. Fathers with ready-made contacts might send sons to learn a trade – as in the case of Thomas Ismay – and later provide the capital to buy a partnership in an existing business. Other firms – like Rankin,

Gilmour and Co. – extended into Liverpool from a base in Glasgow. Yet others, like the Brocklebanks, saw greater opportunities in Liverpool than in Whitehaven and moved the whole business down the coast.

Once wealth had been made, sons and other successors would not normally be educated in Liverpool – the Ismay sons went to Harrow and then Cambridge. Where Sir Edward Bates had his sons educated is not revealed, but it cannot have been in Liverpool since the eldest could be '... met in connection with polo and every kind of fashionable amusement'.[15] After education at local academies became the preserve of the middling and lower ranks of business and the professions in the mid-nineteenth century, any pretension to a more than purely local eminence required education in public schools, and successive generations of the Liverpool aristocracy of commerce were brought up with the national aristocracy of commerce and the landed gentry. The experience of school took the younger generations into social circles with national, European and global connections and these mattered more and more as the most extensive and successful local firms became national and international companies.

Landed wealth plainly provided a model for many new possessors of commercial wealth in the late eighteenth and early nineteenth centuries. Merchants and others in the triangular trade involving slaves and plantation produce made huge fortunes and Liverpool society most certainly did not represent the height of their social ambitions. Writing in 1852, the Revd James Aspinall recalled how in earlier years the Cheshire squires had 'a strong aversion to Liverpool and all its works.' It seems that many of them were mortgaged in Liverpool and:

... they had a sort of prophetic feeling that the
merchant princes of Liverpool were destined to eat
them up ... to buy the acres of all the wiseacres in the
county, and so exterminate the original squirearchy.[16]

In practice it was far more common for the 'merchant
princes' to build new houses in landscaped parklands
than to buy up defaulting squires. By the last quarter
of the nineteenth century the land available on the
Liverpool side of the Mersey for building a stylish new
house had shrunk so much that the Wirral had already
become popular.

In the period of grand house-building which ran for a
century or so – from the late eighteenth to the early
twentieth century – the conception of the appropriate
style was modelled on the 'big house' of the aristocracy
and gentry. In some cases this even included the
attachment of chapel or church to the 'big house', thus
symbolically uniting in the urban 'country estate' the
temporal and spiritual power of rural landowners.
Very few of the urban 'estates' were big enough in
acreage to go to the extent of including a tenanted or
managed model farm, but many did have model
dwellings nearby for their outdoor servants, and a
lodge house or cottage at the main gate was virtually
obligatory. The 'urban estate' was simply a scaled
down version of the country house that had been
popular with the aristocracy since the late seventeenth
century, and no other city saw so many of them (always
excepting London) as Liverpool and its environs.

Ismay's White Star Line ships were famous for their
opulence and the taste revealed in the furnishing and
decor of the ships was also present in the new house
that Ismay had built on the Wirral. A 390-acre estate,
this was one that did come complete with model farm
buildings. Ismay retained these but the house, only

twelve years old, was soon demolished and replaced by
one designed by Norman Shaw, later the architect of
London's New Scotland Yard and the White Star head
office in Liverpool:

> As with everything Thomas Ismay planned, he would
> only have the finest possible material used; in the
> finished house there was not a single nail in the whole
> structure, only the finest brass screws. It was to be a
> reproduction of an Elizabethan manor house, built of a
> red stone quarried locally. It took two years to complete
> ... Tremendous care and thought had gone into the
> building of Dawpool; it was very large, the South front
> overlooking the Dee was over 250 feet long. It cost
> £53,000 to build, an immense sum in those days ... It
> required twenty-two indoor servants and ten outdoor,
> to run it properly. When Mrs. Ismay died in 1907, her
> three sons were each offered it in turn, but they all
> refused to live in it ...[17]

While Ismay was having Dawpool built his partner,
William Imrie, had bought the Homestead, 'a large
stone-built Victorian house, with a massive conserv-
atory, standing in its own ground in Mossley Hill Road,
Liverpool'.[18] Within the decade, one Ismay son had
bought Caldy Manor on the Wirral and another had
bought Sandheys, a large Georgian house with ten
acres on the then rural edge of Liverpool. The great
majority of such semi-stately homes have survived into
other uses ... Sudley, the Holts' family home was left to
the city, complete with much of its art collection. The
MacIver home, Calderstones, with its splendid gardens
and landscaping is Liverpool's most beautiful public
park. Ismay's folly was demolished but his partner's
house remains as a convent. The houses of the
Forwoods and the Brocklebanks and the Mellys and
many others in Liverpool and Wirral have become
schools, colleges, remand homes, the offices of public

companies and public utilities. Together they form a
substantial architectural heritage.

Of course only those who were exceptionally wealthy
could live in the villas and quasi-stately homes on the
rural fringe or further afield, like Dawpool, with a
convenient railway station. An approximation to the
rural ideal was found in the construction of city parks
with large houses built around the edges in curving
tree-lined roads. Part of the mythology of the growth of
public parks in the nineteenth century is that they
were laid out as an amenity for the urban masses.
They were nothing of the kind. The typical nineteenth-
century park was surrounded by very large houses
built for the carriage-owning classes while the parks
themselves were designed to conform with the
favoured rolling parkland idiom of the landed
aristocracy. These parks substituted for the unrealisa-
ble aspirations of those who were nevertheless very
prosperous. No more than a glimpse of Liverpool's city
parks – Newsham, Prince's and Sefton – is needed to
show in the houses of the perimeter and adjacent roads
and streets the domestic architecture of the bourgeoi-
sie. The first public park in Liverpool was Prince's
Park and the land was bought by a property developer
in 1843:

> The outer margins of this plot were reserved for [very
> large] dwelling houses, and the central area was made
> into a park and gardens, for the use of the residents
> and also, under suitable safeguards, for the use of the
> public.[19]

Not until 1918 did this become a *public* park, owned
by the city.

Before substantial improvements in urban commu-
nications and public utilities the prosperous and well

to do mainly lived in the city. Their former presence and the weight of their numbers can still be experienced in the blocks of streets adjacent to the University on one side and the Anglican cathedral and the Polytechnic on another. In this quarter are ranged terrace after terrace of Georgian houses still complete with columned and fanlight doorways and cast-iron balconies. Amongst them are still many grand interiors with wide, curving marble staircases and solid mahogany doors. Outside the squares of London there is no other English town or city – not even Bath – which can show so much outward evidence of late Georgian and Regency architecture. A walk around these streets in an imaginative state of mind is sufficient to dispel all need for statistical proof of Liverpool's wealth in the 1830s and 1840s.

Outward display in commercial architecture came rather later when the leading firms became commercial empires needing cubic footage to house the scores of clerks and the libraries of records, and an impressive façade to convince rivals and the public generally that here was a business to be noticed. In the commercial quarter of the city are the representations in stone, brick and marble of the rise of the company as a *corporate* organisation. In the age of the family firm and the partnership wealth and power were individualised, attached to named persons and visible in their personal consumption. But with the arrival of the limited company public attention had to be drawn to the company itself and so began the change in the visual character of commercial districts. Business was now being conducted from places whose façades were derived from Roman palaces, Greek temples, Rhine castles, chateaux of the Loire, Gothic cathedrals, Byzantine churches. The contrast with earlier business houses was stark, for there it had been common to combine counting house (office) with warehouse in a building that, if decorated in a gesture of detail, was nevertheless purely functional.

The commercial streets of Liverpool still provide enduring and sometimes extravagant evidence of the once locally owned powerful shipping and commercial firms. The public buildings provide even grander confirmation. The greatest monument, St George's Hall, is described by Pevsner as '... the freest neo-Grecian building in England and one of the finest in the world'.[20] Adjacent is another group of neo-Grecian buildings which includes the Walker Art Gallery, erected at the expense of Sir Andrew Walker and which is reckoned to contain the best art collection outside London.

The foreigners who came to Liverpool and made a lot of money were not quite as ungenerous as Orchard suggested. The old Hahnemann Hospital originally endowed by a Liverpool-resident German merchant now provides studios for art students, but in the nearby Women's Hospital the Minoprio Ward, endowed by an expatriate Austrian, still has patients. And only 200 yards away is the large Greek Orthodox Church, endowed among others by the Ralli brothers, the world famous cotton-brokers of Greek origin, and a Mr Papayanni, a Greek shipowner operating from Liverpool and whose line of steamers was sold to Ellerman.

Finally, there is the University whose named buildings and professorships read like a social register, a *Who's Who* of once well known Liverpool merchants, shipowners, landowners and manufacturers.

It is hard to exaggerate the social importance and status that attached to late nineteenth-century philanthropy. The moral of Disraeli's *Sybil* – that property would sensibly recognise duties as well as rights – had apparently been well absorbed by the new rich of commerce and industry. Celebrating Liverpool's old families, and saying how much they deserved the deference given to them, Orchard said:

> Nowhere else in English society is there a larger percentage of chivalric high-mindedness, guided by prudence, of sympathy with friendless talent and steadfast purpose, of recognition that 'property has duties as well as rights', and of readiness to spend time, cash, ability, and influence in working to benefit their inferiors.[21]

So important an index of civic-mindedness was philanthropy that it was thought fair and reasonable to comment on those who were very rich but failed to contribute. Thus Orchard wrote of Sir Edward Bates in 1877:

> He may have been benevolent in secret – I admit the possibility, just as I admit that a comet *may* choke everyone on this earth ... Before the world he was a money-making shipowner and merchant ... and everywhere spoken of with a bitter laugh as hard ...[22]

In their philanthropy as in other matters, the urban commercial rich were once again emulating the ideals of an earlier landowning gentry. By the middle of the nineteenth century the hierarchy of wealth had extended with the growth of the middle class. This new stratum of relative wealth in its turn inevitably emulated those families who in the space of a mere seventy years or so had become the 'old families'. Commenting on this, Hugh Shimmin, a Tory radical who delighted in puncturing pretension, wrote in 1861:

The most fashionable amusement of the present age is philanthropy. Liverpool which delights in following a fashion of any kind, pants and puffs to keep well up with this in especial. But it is a fashion and we would not have the working man suppose that all the gentlemen and ladies of Liverpool ... really do care quite as much about him or understand his condition and his wants quite as well as they give out. No small number of these benevolent persons are philanthropic because it is the fashion to be so; because it brings them into passing contact with this Bishop or that Earl, or even with Mr Cropper or Mr Rathbone, or any other of our leading philanthropists. Not a few ladies, who will visit the garret of a workingman's wife, and talk in the most condescending way, and put on the most friendly interest in the progress of the children, would quiver to the outermost hoops of their crinolines if asked to sit down to tea with the wife of a grocer.[23]

Social science, associated then with philanthropy, also came in for a blast from Shimmin:

Take up social science as nineteen-twentieths of our Liverpool folk do, as something which makes a shopkeeper for a moment hail-fellow with a lord, and flatters an alderman into believing himself a philosopher ... Are you a Liverpool trader? Bring your wife and daughter to the meeting and be sure you are seen shaking hands with Theodore Rathbone ... Once the philanthropist had heavy work, loathsome tasks, public contempt; now he has light and pleasant labour, fashionable honours, the praises of lords, the puffing of newspapers ...[24]

While the middling rich could be legitimately deflated for their use of philanthropy as a badge of prestige, we have already seen how the miserly rich could be publicly despised. Sir Edward Bates was not Orchard's only target. He wrote of Sir William Brown, a millionaire cotton-broker, that while he, Orchard, would have felt keen pleasure in recording Brown's concern for the poor, there was regrettably nothing that could be said and that his '... will ... was universally considered worthy of him who was rumoured to have discharged a footman for having given a plate of broken victuals to a beggar'.[25]

Autocratic tendencies, however, were often admired. Sir William Forwood, himself a shipowner, evidently thought well of the stern discipline exercised by Cunard's Charles MacIver:

> Many stories are told of Mr MacIver's stern discipline. It is said one of his captains asked permission to take his wife to sea with him. Permission was granted, but when the day of sailing arrived he received passenger tickets for himself and his wife, also an intimation that he had been superseded in command of the ship.[26]

A comparable story has also been admiringly told of Thomas Ismay, who was MacIver's great rival:

> Promptly at 8 o'clock T.H. Ismay departed for Liverpool ... if as he walked down the drive, he saw a fallen leaf he placed a stone upon it, and if when he came home in the evening it was still there, he would send for all ten gardeners and demand to know what they had been doing all day.[27]

Not generally admired at all was the philistinism of the rich who were referred to by the Revd James Aspinall as being 'almost a non-reading community'.[28] Hugh Shimmin, himself a self-taught man of working-class origins, was predictably far more scathing:

> Is there any community of civilised men and women in the world where all that pertains to culture of the mind is so little honoured, nay, is so openly scorned, as Liverpool? The pride of ignorance is rampant here. We

say in all sincerity, and without the slightest wish to
exaggerate, that the general public feeling of Liverpool
towards the thinker, the scholar, the man of letters, the
poet, is one of genuine, honest, hearty contempt.[29]

In voicing views of this kind Nathaniel Hawthorne
had been there before Shimmin. In August 1853
Hawthorne went to one of the extravagant dinners
regularly given at the Town Hall to welcome
distinguished visitors:

> The dinner was at the Town Hall; and the rooms, and
> the whole affair, were all in the most splendid style.
> Nothing struck me more than the footmen in the city
> livery; they really looked more magnificent, in their
> gold lace, and breeches, and white silk stockings, than
> any officers of state whom I have ever seen. The rooms
> were beautiful; gorgeously painted and gilded, gor-
> geously lighted, gorgeously hung with paintings,
> gorgeously illuminated – the plate gorgeous, the dinner
> gorgeous in the English fashion. As to the company,
> they had a kind of roughness, that seems to be the
> characteristic of all Englishmen so far as I have yet
> seen them; elderly John Bulls – and there is hardly a
> less beautiful object than the elderly John Bull, with
> his large body, protruding paunch, short legs, and
> mottled, double-chinned, irregular-featured aspect.
> They are men of the world, at home in society, easy in
> their manners, but without refinement; nor are they
> especially what one thinks of, under the appellation of
> gentleman.[30]

Hawthorne's complaint about the lack of gentlemen
was extended to the Derbys – substantial landowners,
established aristocracy and by the late nineteenth
century regarded in local society as inviolate. But in
1854, at least, the Derbys were not liked and were
accused by their neighbours and the Liverpool gentry

as of 'arrogant and unsocial habits'. Moreover, says Hawthorne:

> ... all those centuries do not seem to have made the race truly noble, or else it has latterly degenerated; for the present Lord Stanley, a young man of twenty-six, eldest son of the Earl, is said to be a mean fellow. There is a story (averred to be true, though only mentioned in a whisper) that, while at Rugby School, he stole a five-pound note, and, I think, was compelled to leave the school for it. In his present character so far as I can understand, there is nothing to obliterate this early stain.[31]

The United States' Consul had been no more impressed with the Bramley-Moores who if striving for 'old family' status, had not in 1854 achieved it:

> On the whole, the dinner was not a very agreeable one. I led in Mrs Bramley-Moore (the only lady present) and found her a stupid woman, of vulgar tone, and outrageously religious – even to the giving away of little tracts, and lending religious books. The family are virulent Tories, fanatics for the Established Church, and followers of Dr McNeille, who is the present low church Pope of Liverpool. I could see little to distinguish her from a rigidly orthodox and Calvinistic woman of New England ... The eatables and drinkables were very praiseworthy; and Mr Bramley-Moore circulated his wines more briskly than is customary at gentlemen's tables. He, too, I suspect, is not quite a gentleman; not of one of those ancient merchant-princely families, who form the century-old aristocracy of Liverpool ... He seems to be rich, however, has property in the Brazils ... has been Mayor of Liverpool ... and now lives at a very pretty place. But he alludes to the cost of wines, and of other things which he possesses; a frailty which I have not observed in any other Englishman of good station ... he seems to be a passably good man; but I hope, on the whole, that

he will not ask me to dinner any more – though his dinners are certainly very good.[32]

Hawthorne was writing at mid-century and for his private notebooks. Orchard, by contrast, was writing fifty years later and for the public. By this time robust words were more often applied to reputations when the victim was safely dead. At his most bitingly eloquent, Orchard said of R.A. MacFie:

> ... sugar refiner, millionaire, social magnate, Presbyterian busybody, member of the Imperial Legislature was ... not quite the giant of intellect he would have the world believe him. Clever in a sense he undoubtedly was, for during many years he managed a refinery so enormous that I scarcely dare to say how many hundreds of workmen there earned their living, and a business so widespread that its operations extended all over Europe. But apart from the influence this secured, he was merely a sensible gentleman and a great bore. Fond of speaking as he was, even the most patient listeners fled in terror from his orations.[33]

By the 1890s understandings and definitions had changed and it would not then have occurred to Orchard to question MacFie's status as a gentleman. Hawthorne however, had resorted to an older usage where gentlemen were those who had had some education, acquired cultural aspirations and at least some intellectual interests. Hawthorne himself was a man of the world and an intellectual – and disappointedly found few like himself in the social circles he was obliged to inhabit. Excepting the Rathbones, who from the late eighteenth century had regularly renewed intellectual interests in each generation, Liverpool's rich were no less and no more than those elsewhere given to a disinterested pursuit of scientific or artistic knowledge.

The wealthy of Liverpool, like their metropolitan counterparts, were not distinguished for their intellectual qualities nor for their appreciation of the arts. But they were, nevertheless, highly sensitive to the status significance of scarce objects. When Thomas Ismay refused an increase in his commission from grateful shareholders in 1881, he did agree to sit to Millais for his portrait and to accept a silver gilt dinner service that was 'three years in the manufacturers' hands – thanks to its complex and ornate character – [and] cost over four thousand guineas'.[34]

The centrepiece of this dinner service represented an astonishing piece of impertinence that was completely in character. It featured a globe around which were seated the figures of four great navigators – Jason (of Greek mythology), da Gama, Colombus and Cook. Then, as if to link the White Star Line and Ismay himself to the accomplishments of the four explorers, '... two of the four panels behind the figures of the great navigators are engraved with the official seal of the Oceanic Steam Navigation Co. and Mr Ismay's crest ...'[35]

Twelve months before this presentation in 1885 the Revd Acland Armstrong arrived in Liverpool to be minister to the wealthy Unitarian congregation in Hope Street and later recalled:

I came to Liverpool a stranger some six or seven years ago, knowing only that I was about to take up my residence in the second city of the mightiest Empire the world has ever seen. I admired its public buildings, its vast docks, its stately shipping, its splendid shops, its lovely parks. It seemed to me that this was a city in which one might be proud to be a citizen; a city which must be administered and governed by men of high capacity and generous temper.

But after the first glance I was appalled by one

aspect of things here which pressed on my mind more
and more for several weeks, till the sin of it became at
times well nigh unbearable. The contiguity of immense
wealth and abysmal poverty forced itself upon my
notice. The hordes of the ragged and the wretched
surged up from their native quarters and covered the
noblest streets like a flood. Men and women in the
cruellest grip of poverty, little children with shoeless
feet, bodies pinched and faces in which the pure light of
childhood had been quenched, swarmed on the
pavements that fronted the most brilliant shops; and
the superb carriages of the rich, with their freights of
refined and elegant ladies, threaded their way among
sections of the population so miserable and squalid
that my heart ached at the sight of them. I had seen
wealth. I had seen poverty. But never before had I seen
the two so jammed together.[36]

These sorts of contrasts between rich and poor as well
as the detail of city poverty were familiar to the
Victorian rich and middle classes. These worst aspects
of urban social conditions were regularly – and often
melodramatically – exposed in local newspapers and
journals, in the reports of Medical Officers of Health,
relief organisations, Royal Commissions and Select
Committees, the novels of Dickens and Gissing, the
drawings of Doré in the *Illustrated London News*. No
one who was literate and took a minimal, passing
interest in the world could not know. And yet, as the
Revd Armstrong put it, conscience was unawakened.

A survey in 1873 showed that of a possible 20,000
contributors to charity in Liverpool, only 6,688
actually contributed and of those 1,193 gave more than
half the total. General conditions in Liverpool could
not have appreciably improved in the following ten
years for in 1883 the *Liverpool Daily Post* commented:
'Liverpool has throughout the last forty years stood, as
she stands today, supreme in the black list.'[37] There is

no reason to suppose that the rich of Liverpool were any less generous than the rich elsewhere. What made Liverpool distinctively bad was the scale of the poverty and the irregularity of port and port-related employments.

In truth, the scale of poverty was far beyond the reach of private charity. Intervention by local and central government through general taxation was the only possible way – and the rich of Liverpool were among the first to recognise this. Mr A.B. Forwood, Tory Mayor of Liverpool and shipowner, was an early advocate of council housing, having arrived at the view that private enterprise was incapable of providing a reasonable standard of housing at a rent the poor could afford to pay. Faced with the political awakening of the poorer urban masses in the 1890s and 1900s, the final recognition of the hopeless inadequacy of private philanthropy came quickly. Benefactions and endowments remained common enough but were devoted mainly to promoting the arts and youth organisations and expressed an individual commitment rather than one imposed by the elite. Subscription lists and attendances at meetings promoting 'good causes' were no longer an index of prestige to be carefully reported in the local journals. In other ways, too, 'Liverpool society' gradually dropped out of view. Congregations of the rich and powerful at churches disintegrated. Assembly Room balls vanished and daughters 'came out' in London, no longer in the Wellington Rooms. Town Hall dinners now marked only the rituals of the calendar of state and monarchy. 'Stately homes' on the city's edge became schools or convents. Big houses on park perimeters converted to nursing homes, student residences, flats, clubs and, very occasionally, brothels. The rituals and observances involved in the display of local power mattered for as long as the wealthy and

powerful families needed Liverpool. As soon as the
local dynasties – new and old alike – were overtaken by
larger currents of change in the economic system of
Britain and the world, then so did 'Liverpool society'
decay and disintegrate.

'Names' lingered. Lawrence Holt, nephew of Alfred,
was still active in the business and on the magistrates'
bench in the 1950s; Eleanor Rathbone was MP for the
Northern Universities in the 1930s; another and more
reputable Lord Derby was recruited to be Lord Mayor
for Coronation year in 1953; the Bates and Brocklebanks were important in the affairs of Cunard until
long after the end of the Second World War. Newer
shipping wealth, represented by the de Larrinagas of
Spanish origin, only sold up in the 1970s with the
marquee for the auction provided by Christies. Old
names linger in connection with the governing bodies
of the University and the Liverpool Council for
Voluntary Service. There is even a 'new' name – the
Moore family who own the Littlewoods oganisation.
The firm is now headed by the Eton-educated, second
generation John Moore. The senior John Moore, in his
nineties, followed the line laid down by the old
families: he is a world famous patron of modernism in
art and a generous supporter of local liberal causes.

The basis of local power wielded by the 'old families'
and their newer but equally wealthy colleagues was
not a function of superlative personal qualities. Few
were gentlemen in the sense of the term used by
Hawthorne. Some were unscrupulous, like Sir Alfred
Jones in his attempt to cover up Belgian atrocities in
the Congo.[38] The other well known shipping knight, Sir
Edward Bates, was notorious for sending poorly
equipped ships to sea and ill-treating his crews.[39] For
their part, the 'old families' could claim an earlier
William Rathbone who had refused to sell timber for the

construction of ships that were to be used in the slave trade.[40]

Questions of principle and scruple, philanthropy and artistic sensitivity did matter – and transgressors were always needed to highlight the virtues of others. Philanthropic displays, especially collective ones, represented an adherence to high moral values. Lack of 'gentility' was not a handicap when so few others either had it or aspired to it – and anyway it could be hidden behind the consumption of precious art objects or in the endowment of a university professorship. Against all this, the miserly, the philistine and the unscrupulous might then be used to illustrate the general excellence of the donors who represented the positive human values. It is everywhere a feature of the powerful that they attempt to legitimate their coercive power by clothing themselves in moral and personal superiority. The wealthy of Liverpool were no exception.

The giant company with a cobweb-fine network of subsidiaries scattered over the globe and a turnover comparable to the income of a middle-ranking nation is now, in the late twentieth century, a familiar and largely unremarked phenomenon. One hundred years earlier large companies with integrated operations which looked like miniature nation states were a novelty. This new type of company was first seen in its modern form in the liner companies of Liverpool and London. Fleets of expensive steamers running to schedules needed good cargoes to make them pay – and so the shipping companies integrated chains of agencies to find the cargoes and wharves, lighters and feeder services to get them to the ships. The capital needed to construct a company of this type could no longer so readily be found from within the family or the partnership. Companies like Cunard and Alfred Holt's were, accordingly, regularly reconstructed so as to enlarge the capital base. Eventually, this meant becoming public companies although family control was usually retained through large blocks of shareholdings.[41] The enlargement of the firm and the input of new capital frequently meant that the original partners could not find enough relatives to manage the business and so began the employment of professional managers with an equivalence of power to family members. In firms like Alfred Holt's there was obviously an expectation that senior managers would take on civic responsibility, hence Sydney Jones's term as Lord Mayor early in the Second World War, but this was not normal elsewhere. Professional managers were oriented to their company careers rather than to civic duty.

In the end, it was the logic of the development of the capitalist economy and its typical corporate form rather than personal failings or limitations which led to the obliteration of the 'old families' as a major force in Liverpool. But the rhetoric they used to extol the city and its world role passed to others whose livelihood in the city was dependent upon a continuation of its traditional role as a port. The sense of stature that Liverpool people have of themselves is due in part to the extravagant language once used so readily and frequently by the 'old families'.

Notes

1 For this and the preceding data on the regional distribution of wealth, see W.D. Rubinstein, 'The Victorian Middle Classes: Wealth, Occupation and Geography', *Economic History Review*, Second Series, Vol. XXX, 1977, pp.602-23. Also, W.D. Rubinstein, 'Wealth, Elites and the Class Structure of Modern Britain', *Past and Present*, No.76, 1977.

2 B.G. Orchard, *Liverpool's Legion of Honour*, Liverpool 1893.
3 See: F.E. Hyde, *Blue Funnel*, Liverpool 1956; F.E. Hyde, *Shipping Enterprise and Management, 1830–1939, Harrisons of Liverpool*, Liverpool 1967; F.E. Hyde, *Cunard and the North Atlantic, 1840–1973*, London 1975.
4 Orchard, op.cit., p.121.
5 P.N. Davies, *Sir Alfred Jones*, London 1978, pp.60-1.
6 Hyde, *Blue Funnel*, Chapters 5, 6 and 7.
7 Sheila Marriner and F.E. Hyde, *The Senior John Samuel Swire*, Liverpool 1967, p.12.
8 Quoted in Thomas Kelly, *For the Advancement of Learning*, Liverpool 1981, pp.47-8.
9 Ibid., p.69-70.
10 M.J. Daunton, *Coal Metropolis*, Leicester 1977, p.52.
11 Orchard, op.cit., p.22.
12 Davies, op.cit., p.76.
13 See T.S. and M.B. Simey, *Charles Booth*, London 1960, p.39.
14 Ibid., pp.60-1.
15 Orchard, op.cit., p.155.
16 'An Old Stager' (James Aspinall), *Liverpool a Few Years Since*, Liverpool 1885, p.57.
17 Wilton J. Oldham, *The Ismay Line*, Liverpool 1961, pp.68-9.
18 Ibid., p.68.
19 Kelly, op.cit., p.29
20 Pevsner, op.cit., p.155.
21 Orchard, op.cit., p.23.
22 Ibid., pp.152ff.
23 Quoted in M.B. Simey, *Charitable Effort in Liverpool in the Nineteenth Century*, Liverpool 1951, p.56.
24 Ibid., pp.56-7.
25 Orchard, op.cit., p.215.
26 Sir William B. Forwood, *Reminiscences of a Liverpool Shipowner*, Liverpool 1920, pp.35-6.
27 Oldham, op.cit., p.110.
28 'An Old Stager', op.cit., p.95.
29 Quoted in M.B. Simey, op.cit., p.14.
30 Nathaniel Hawthorne, *The English Notebooks*, New York 1941, p.12.
31 Ibid., p.53.
32 Ibid., pp.55-6.
33 Orchard, op.cit., p.475.
34 Oldham, op.cit., p.78.
35 Ibid., p.79.
36 Quoted in M.B. Simey, op.cit., p.98.
37 Ibid., p.99.
38 Davies, op.cit., pp.121-3.

39 Sir Edward Bates in British Parliamentary Papers, *Correspond-ence between the Board of Trade or other Bodies or Persons on the Subject of Scurvy in Merchant Ships*, 1871 (434), pp.52-3.
40 Eric Williams, *Capitalism and Slavery*, London 1964, pp.58-9
41 See Hyde, *Blue Funnel* and *Cunard and the North Atlantic*.

3 Natural Democrats

Democratic sentiments seemed to flower everywhere in Britain in the 1960s. Northern provincial cities were being 'discovered' by metropolitan cultural arbiters, class barriers were apparently being dissolved and suddenly it was acceptable to be assertively and unashamedly Northern and working class. Those who were conspicuously dressed and accented in the clothes and mannerisms of traditional authority were as often likely to be ridiculed as to receive automatic respect and genuflection. The symbols and badges of authority were no longer enough. It was now necessary to provide proof of competence and merit.

A certain scepticism toward authority and a general independent-mindedness was consistent with what had been, for many decades, the natural disposition of the people living in the waterfront districts of Liverpool. Nathaniel Hawthorne had scarcely been six months in Liverpool when, in 1854, he was remarking on the independence of the working people he saw:

> Aboard the ferry-boat yesterday, a labouring man eating oysters; he took them, one by one from his pocket in interminable succession, opened them with his jacknife, swallowed the oyster, threw the shell overboard – and then for another. Having concluded his meal, he took out a clay tobacco pipe, filled, lighted it with a rush, and smoked it, all this while the other passengers were looking at him, and with a perfect coolness and independence, such as no single man can ever feel in America. Here, a man does not seem to consider what other people will think of his conduct, but whether it suits his convenience to do so and so.[1]

In 1983, and as if to confirm and enlarge upon Hawthorne's observations, a captain of a Liverpool liner company gave his opinion of Liverpool seamen:

> I like their sense of humour – they'll take the mickey out of anybody. They're no respecters of rank – of the person, yes, but the rank, no. The fact that you've got gold bars on your sleeve doesn't mean anything, it's whether you're good at your job that counts. If you are, then that's alright.[2]

The habit of mind glancingly noticed by Hawthorne and more comprehensively rubbed into the experience of many more ship's masters than the one quoted here, were a product of the utterly distinctive way of life that waterfront Liverpudlians had developed in their own defence.

In the middle of the nineteenth century the old families and those aspiring to the same status had

moved up to the ridge overlooking the city. The narrow
plain, following the course of the river and adjacent to
the docks, became working-class territory which
commerce and industry only occupied by day. Before
the end of the century the 'respectable' working class of
artisans and the regularly employed had also been
moved and segregated – into geometrically neat rows
of streets of new terraces conforming to regulations
framed to promote public health. The courts, alleys
and narrow, chasmed streets of dockland became the
domain and the region of the casually employed.
Crammed haphazardly into a maze of streets
containing mills and refineries, workshops and stables,
warehouses and breweries, almost one quarter of a
million people lived here in 1901. Here was a city
within a city and one that was equivalent in size to
Bristol or Newcastle-upon-Tyne.[3]

The citizens of the waterfront had in common a close
association with ships and ocean commerce, incomes
similar enough to promote a rough and ready
egalitarianism and a widely shared distrust of any of
the agents sent into their domain by the 'other
Liverpool'. Relieving officers and their National
Assistance Board successors, police and officials of the
city council were uniformly regarded with the deepest
suspicion. Through parental warnings and conversa-
tions overhead, children learned early that honourable
people avoided contact with authority's agents or
stonewalled them when questioning was inescapable.

Although the dockland population was unified by its
system of ethics, customs and interlocking networks of
neighbouring allegiances, there were also – as one
would expect to find in any city – divisions based upon
ethnicity, religion, parish, occupation and industry.
Dockland people, furthermore, were not entirely cut off
from the 'respectable' working class whose streets

everywhere marked the limits of the other Liverpool. There were always the changes in economic circumstances producing migrations both inwards and outwards as well as the connections made through family and workplace. But with the Liverpool of the old families the only connections were political. These will be looked at in the next chapter.

Port economies have always been distinctive, and the essential nature of Liverpool's at its Edwardian peak is well caught in Ramsay Muir's description:

> There is probably no city of anything like equal size in which so small a proportion of the population is maintained by permanent and stable industrial work. There are, of course, a number of minor industries carried on in the town, but of these, some (such as matchmaking) depend upon low-paid and comparatively unskilled labour. And the principal occupation of the city, the foundation of its prosperity, is the handling of goods between ship, warehouse and railway; a function which is mainly performed by unskilled labour. And as this work comes largely in sudden rushes, and has to be done at high pressure in order to save interest on costly ships and costly dock space and warehouse space, it has come about that a large proportion of the men employed have no permanent work, but must submit to periods of idleness alternating with periods of sudden heavy labour, extending over long hours ... Thus the great development of steamships and dock has brought it about that the city's prosperity largely depends upon casual labour, the most degrading as well as the most insecure form of employment; and that Liverpool has to deal with a social problem perhaps more acute than that which faces any other city.[4]

While Muir was talking mainly of dock labourers, he could easily have been talking of a much wider range of occupations. A 1929 study conducted for the Ministry

of Labour listed 28 industrial sectors as employers of
casual labour and identified 231 separate call-on
points or stands along the seven miles of the
waterfront.[5]

In the normal pattern of work for a casual worker
the period of hire lasted as long as the job. The seafarer
was hired by the voyage, the docker for the time taken
to load or discharge a cargo, the ship-repair worker for
the time taken to complete a specific task. The
following account of Albert Rose's work as a shipwright
in the 1930s provides an excellent example of how the
system worked:

> All the work on the ships was casual and there weren't
> that many ships around at that time. The different
> firms, like Harrison's, Elder Dempster's, Evans',
> Grayson's all had their stands at different places on the
> dock road. The labourers would be in one place,
> boilermakers in another, shipwrights in another, and
> there would be joiners and fitters as well. If there was
> no work going at one stand then you would be *running*
> to the next, carrying your box of tools. At the other
> stand it was nothing out of the way for four or five men
> out of fifty to get on that day. I was working like that
> for three years until I got taken on permanently by
> Mersey Docks and Harbour Board. I'd be on the stand
> at seven-thirty every morning and then again at one
> o'clock and sometimes again at three in case they were
> calling on for a start the next day.
>
>   Sometimes, I'd have several different jobs in the one
> day. I'd get one at seven-thirty and get finished at
> eleven. Then perhaps the chargehand would say there
> might be something this afternoon so I'd get on again at
> one and perhaps work till four. There was many a week
> when I'd get only a half-day in, a day, or one-and-a-half
> days. In fact it was like that more often than not. It was
> nothing out of the way to be working for two different
> firms in one day. If you happened to have a good week
> you could easily have worked for five different firms.
> The longest I ever worked in those three years was for

three weeks when I touched out lucky for a ship that had come in for a survey refit. The only other job that you could rely on for a longish spell was if a ship needed a big recaulking job: recaulking the fo'c'sle head, the bridge, the boat deck and the poop could last ten days. If you got a full week in you'd get about £3 but that didn't happen too often. More often it was a few hours work in one week and for that I might get as little as 5s 3d [26p].

Of course we had our ways of finding out what work there was likely to be. If there was no work at seven-thirty you'd go to the Cocoa Rooms to have a cup of tea and read the *Journal of Commerce* because that had all the details of the shipping movements. Most fellers would go to the Regulating Office in the Dock Board Building at the Pierhead. In a basement window on the South side there was a slate saying if there were any movements due at the graving docks. It might say, for example, that a Harrison boat, say the *Explorer*, was going to be docked by Grayson's for four days at Herculaneum and then off you'd go to Grayson's stand. If you got on for docking a ship then you also had the privilege of taking her out and so altogether that would be a full day's work. Of course you would only get on for the docking and undocking – it didn't mean that you would necessarily get to work on her while she was in.[6]

That account of casual labour in the ship-repair trades could equally represent the pattern of work for dockers, carters, warehousemen as well as labourers in marshalling yards, mills and sugar refineries. The pattern for seafarers was quite different. If sailing on regular Liverpool traders the period of engagement would be known in advance. Voyages in the mid-1960s were similar in duration to those in the 1900s: seven weeks for a round trip to the Eastern Mediteranean, three months to West Africa, Brazil or the Caribbean and as long as five months on refrigerated ships to Australian ports. On a tramp steamer it might be six weeks if it was carrying grain from Canada and as long as two years if the ship got a series of charters that kept it away from the United Kingdom or Northern Europe. Seafaring employment was obviously not casual on the same day-to-day basis as it was for dockers and others, but there was still no continuity of employment. The only ships with regular crews were those on the North Atlantic passenger runs, but even there crews were discharged and unpaid for the week or so they were in Liverpool before sailing on the next voyage.

By no means everyone working in port industry was casually employed. The railway goods yards and depots had their regularly employed drivers, guards and clerks, and most of the Dock Board's 5,000-strong workforce of the skilled shipyard trades, dockgatemen and crews of dredgers and floating cranes were permanent employees. The mills and refineries all kept regular staff, as did the shipping companies with their shore gangs who minded the ships while they were in port. They and many other regularly employed were the elite who lived in the streets of the 'respectable' working class. But it was the casual section whose economic and social influence most influenced the city's culture.

The precise extent of casual labour in Liverpool or anywhere else in the UK has never, at any time, been known. The nearest estimate was provided by the Census of 1921 which gave the numbers of workers who reported having no fixed workplace. The resulting figures are used here as an indication of the extent of casual employment even though they exclude seafarers away on voyage. The table overleaf provides an illustration of how different were the labour markets of port compared with manufacturing towns. For example, Bootle, economically and socially an integral part of the Liverpool dockland, had twelve times more men without a fixed workplace than the coal and glass town of St Helens, just twelve miles inland.

Male Workers Without Fixed Workplaces in Port and Manufacturing Towns, 1921

Ports	Percentage	Manufacturing Towns	Percentage
Liverpool	20	Manchester	5
Bootle	25	St Helens	2
London – Stepney	15	London – Fulham	7
South Shields	16	Gateshead	5
Hull	20	Wakefield	5
Cardiff	20	Ebbw Vale	1

Source: Census, 1921, (Workplaces, Table 1)

Casual labour meant irregular and uncertain income which, in turn, meant regular contact with poverty. In the nineteenth century Liverpool was notorious for its squalor, for epidemic diseases and high death rates. Liverpool was the first British city to appoint a Medical Officer of Health (in 1847) and among the very first to build council housing (St Martin's Cottages, 1869). Both developments represented recognition of a desperate state of affairs rather than progressive politics.

The squalor that attracted most attention was in the dockland districts. In 1880 some 70,000 people were living in court houses that had been condemned as unfit for habitation.[7] In 1882 the new Medical Officer of Health (MOH) said that whole districts were 'plagued as the cholera-smitten cities of India'.[8] Yet another

MOH, this time in 1906, continued to report dreadful conditions. Speaking to a meeting of the City Council's Health Committee, he said: '... there was not a city in this country, nay in Europe, which could produce anything like the squalor that his officials found in some of Liverpool's backstreets.'[9]

In 1905 Burlington Street, a typical locality in the South Scotland ward, recorded more deaths from dysentery than any street in the city. In the following year the average death rate in the street was 44.0 per 1,000 compared with a city average of 20.6.[10] The street was typical of the area – business premises fronting on to the street and court housing, down narrow entries, off it. In 1909 the only listed occupations were of seamen and carters. On the street itself were a jumble of workshops – a chairmaker, a broom-maker, a handcart hirer and repairer, a saddler. There were also some larger businesses – a dry-salter, a sugar refiner, a miller, a seed-crusher, a manufacturing chemist, a sack merchant and a warehousing firm. To add to the health hazards of some of these businesses there was also at least one stable for horses and two shippons for cows. Ministering to the ill-health of the street were a herbalist and a dispensary of the Liverpool Medical Missionary Society where treatment could be had for a penny or even free of charge. For those of the local residents who had managed to acquire anything of value but were periodically hard-up, there were two pawnbrokers.[11]

The shops in the poorest streets naturally sold goods commensurate with the incomes of the inhabitants. The following description was reported in the *Liverpool Review* in 1899:

Many of the quondam drawing rooms have been turned into the show windows of filthily untidy hucksters' shops, where fat, sweaty cheese and oily pieces of bacon

are exposed for sale, surrounded by a hotchpotch of
stale sweets, 'speckled apples', Epsom salts, hair oil,
ha'penny toys, unwholesome looking potted herrings
and many other commodities of a cheap and nasty
nature. Other windows do duty as wardrobe shops ...
Second-hand shops, exposing for sale furniture almost
past firewood use, cracked crocks and discarded
culinary utensils, pictures of our Saviour and the
Virgin ornately decorated wth tinsel ornaments,
vermin-infested mattresses ...[12]

While the living conditions associated with low and
unpredictable incomes were undoubtedly bad, the
most abject state of poverty and the most capricious
terms of the labour market were not shared by
everyone. Casual employments were not equally
casual. The most casually employed were dock
labourers, but even here the matter of getting work
was not entirely a lottery. The foreman at the stands
did not blindly pick each man according to his youth
and physique, but the bribing of foremen with ale is
unlikely to have been as widespread as oral legend has
it. Religious allegiance was certainly a potent factor in
some places and in some trades. In the South End
docks where Protestant and Catholic territories
overlapped, membership of one or the other could
make the difference between work or no work. Orange
Lodge influence was reckoned strong among the
carters in most areas of the North docks as well as in
the ship-repair trades. More generally, family connection, membership of parish organisation or other local
association could offer at least some protection from
otherwise wholly unpredictable employment. The first
major survey of dockers' earnings, in 1913, showed 40
per cent getting more than £1 per week and there must
have been a sizeable minority of dockers who, while
working casually, earned enough to avoid living in the
very worst conditions.[13]

Seafarers, we have already noticed, were often
employed for months at a time and in periods between
ships it was customary for them to work in one or other
of the casual trades. Seafarers, however, were paid
monthly while at sea and were also restricted in the
proportion of their wages they could allot to their
dependents. Already low-waged, many seafarers'
families lived more precariously than the regularity of
employment might suggest. The following case
brought to public notice by Eleanor Rathbone, provides
an excellent example:

> Mrs D is ... a fireman's wife, but her husband, as she
> proudly told us, is 'one of the best'. She considers
> herself a lucky woman, yet this is how she has to
> manage: his voyages last six months, and his outfit
> swallows up a great part of the month's advance note of
> £4 10s. She has paid as much as 2s 3d to the
> moneylender for cashing it. [Shipowners never
> advanced cash, T.L.] While waiting till the first
> half-pay allotment of £2 5s becomes due, eight weeks
> after he has sailed, she works at a jam factory, leaving
> her four children ... in the care of her mother ... She lets
> the rent run on, pawns and goes on credit, secure that
> when her husband returns these debts will be paid and
> the furniture redeemed.[14]

The maintenance of family income was the critical
thing for the casually employed and the paid work
done by women was extremely important in each
succeeding generation. The following example comes
from the mid-1930s and was given by a docker who was
recalling his early teens when his father, a seaman,
was unemployed:

> My mother had a handcart and she used to sell toffee
> apples and potted herrings. I'd push it for her when I
> came home from school. I'd leave school at a

quarter-to-twelve to pick up my mother at Beamish
Street wash-house – my mother took in washing as
well as doing the handcart business. We also sold toffee
apples and potted herrings from the house.

My old girl's toffee apples were quite something –
she'd sell 300 on a Saturday afternoon at a ha'penny
apiece. She'd pot her own herrings as well. She'd boil
up the vinegar with various pickling things and then
put this in big jars with the herrings. Our lobby was
always full up with toffee apples and jars of herrings.[15]

Whether it was working as a trader, taking in
laundry, keeping a lodger or mending sacks and bags
in a warehouse, income from one or several of these
could be essential. However, these contributions to the
household economy were as uncertain as those made
by men. For women, as for men, there were very few
opportunities for regular, waged labour.

Where irregular and insufficient male wages could
be supplemented or exceeded by women's earnings and
where casual employment was not entirely erratic,
then escape from the worst of poverty was possible.
The docklands were not homogeneous, either in the
quality of the housing or in the range of incomes. It
was true that a very high proportion of Liverpool's
worst housing was in docklands but never at any one
time between 1900 and 1980 had *all* the housing in
those districts been condemned as unfit. What, for
example, was regarded as relatively good housing in
1910 was only condemned in the 1950s. Where
differences in income were concerned, a prosperous
outsider would have found the distinctions between
the almost poor, the poor and the very poor extremely
marginal. And so they were. But those margins
mattered to families and individuals who might in one
lifetime move up and down that cruelly short scale
several times. The organisation and management of

survival was, of course, done by women. Teenage boys and men, for their part, could escape to the ships.

Until the 1960s British children learned in their schools about the wonders and the size of the British Empire. Since the 1870s successive generations of Liverpool's dockland children had grown familiar with the sight of some of Empire's overseas citizens and, above all, with the names and the liveries of the ships that brought imperial commerce literally to their doorsteps. Half-way up many of the steeply rising streets of the South End, the funnels of Harrison's and Elder Dempster ships were no less visible in 1965 than they had been in 1895. And where ships were hidden by warehouses and mills, the sounds of ships and the smells of their cargoes were blown through the streets by the wind off the river.

From a childhood spent in this environment it was inevitable that boys and young men should follow other members of their families and embark upon a seagoing career. John Dooligan, who sailed on his first voyage in the 1930s, was impelled by a set of experiences that were substantially the same as thousands who had gone before and thousands who would follow:

In those days most of the people I lived by were seamen. I was brought up with ships or something to do with ships – the docks. Then as kids we used to play around the docks and sneak in and then get chased out by the police. The Pierhead in Liverpool was my playground. There used to be a line of ships which you could see looking out of our window; you could see Cammell Laird's. I was living almost right on the dock road. Most of my 'education' was on ships. By the time I was twelve I knew every shipping company by the colour of their funnels. And then when I was fourteen I

went scaling, boiler-scaling – you had to be little to get
in and when I went on the ships it got me thinking
about going away to sea. It wasn't the idea of travel – I
just thought it was a man's job. Most of my friends
went away as well ... [16]

Tony Santamera, who sailed on his first voyage as a
galley boy in 1960, underlines the continuity of
experience:

As far back as I can remember I wanted to go to sea. I'd
never wanted to do anything else. There was the idea of
travel and right back as far as I can remember there
was always sea-talk. There would be parties in the
house and there were always seamen who came and
then people would drop in who'd just come back fom a
trip – and then there were always letters coming in. All
we ever heard in the house was about ships and the sea
and I didn't know about anything else. I was born in
Windsor Gardens which is only about a ten-minute
walk from the docks and then we moved to Great
Crosshall Street which again is only about ten minutes
from the Pierhead. My father often used to take me
down to the docks and to ships that he was on and
when I got older I was always down the docks with my
mates after the nuts, fruit and brown sugar. [17]

The tendency of sons to follow their fathers to sea was
a well established pattern and had been picked up by
the Merseyside Social Survey, in the 1930s. A
comparison of nine different occupations showed
seamen's sons more likely to follow their fathers (one
in four) than the sons of any other group. [18]

Seafaring was a young man's occupation and few
stayed at sea for a working lifetime. A major study of
British seamen in 1961 showed that 70 per cent of new
entrants were under twenty-one and that half left the
sea within two years, 75 per cent within five years and
90 per cent within ten years. [19] Although the earlier

statistics are not so complete, the pattern is consistent with what is known of nineteenth-century seafarers. 40 per cent of merchant seamen were under twenty-five years of age in 1851 and 35 per cent were under twenty-five in 1968.[20] A combination of high labour turnover and a large number of men serving as seamen at any one time meant that in the Liverpool docklands an extraordinary proportion of men had been away to sea at one time or another.

The continual influx of seamen into port employments and the regular arrivals and departures of those still at sea infused into dockland Liverpool a distinctive set of habits and an outlook that harmonised with a community accustomed to uncertainty and casual labour. If seamen bought home with them a certain spice of adventure, sometimes they also brought with them a substantial pay-off; an accumulation of earnings enforced by a lengthy sea passage. This was money to be spent immediately. In this community where planning and foresight were just so much wasted effort, riches, no matter how small, were for immediate consumption. Moments were to be seized and wrung dry. All of this, the 'spice' and the big spend, are evoked in Joseph McKeown's recollection of his Uncle Mick returning home to Birkenhead in the 1930s with Archie, his shipmate:

... during the brief span of his first visit [Archie] taught me how to splice a rope, spit downwind, sew buttons, press trousers, make a pancake and a dozen other things. He took me down to the docks and for the first time, though I had been born among ships, I really saw them ... In his slow deliberate way, he turned every ship we passed into a magic carpet to anywhere in the world, and I became the envy of the gang ... With the true gift of the wanderer he settled down amongst us as though he had known us all his life. Both he and Uncle

Mick, with pocketsfull after a long voyage, seemed determined to sail as flat-broke as possible on the following Saturday. Every night became a party night and I slept when and where I could as the house rocked to the wail of the concertina and sea shanty. Within forty-eight hours Uncle Mick's bounding spirit brought us the first of two visits from Lofty Rourke, the tall rangy policeman ...[21]

And as John Cornelius remembers his part of Liverpool, habits had not changed in the 1960s:

In those days lots of kids' Dads were sailors. Away for months, even a year or more, then all of a sudden coming home like a conquering hero, laden with presents ... African masks, bamboo whistles, that didn't whistle ... Slamming taxi doors hard, dashing the driver a fiver. Very impressive. And loads of money![22]

And they were still the same in the 1970s. J.M.M. Hill reports a seafarer saying of the rapid turnaround of container ships that in port the crew were 'five minute millionaires' and quotes a young deck hand as saying: 'When you go home you're a big time Scottie and then quite quickly the money disappears and you decide you had better go back again to get more ...'[23] Remarks of this sort immediately reach back to Melville's sailortown Liverpool of the 1830s.

In the evening, especially when the sailors are gathered in great numbers, these streets present a most singular spectacle, the entire population of the vicinity being seemingly turned into them. Hand-organs, fiddles and cymbals, plied by strolling musicians, mix with the songs of the seamen ... From the various boarding-houses, each distinguished by gilded emblems outside – an anchor, a crown, a ship, a windlass, or a dolphin – proceeds the noise of revelry and dancing; and from the open casements lean young girls and old women, chattering and laughing with the crowds in the middle of the street. Every moment strange greetings are exchanged between old sailors who chance to stumble upon a shipmate, last seen in Calcutta or Savannah; and the invariable courtesy that takes place upon these occasions, is to go to the next spirit-vault and drink each other's health.[24]

A less innocent account of another place and another time was consistent with what Melville omitted. The following story was told by Frank Fearon, describing events on his first trip to sea in 1965 when he was sixteen and had only just left school:

I stayed ashore [in Valparaiso] for four days. I was in the bar all day and then at night one of the women would take me back to her little flat. When I got home and told my friends what had happened they wouldn't have it, they thought I was telling a load of lies. But if you were a kid down there with blue eyes you couldn't go wrong with women. I mean, that was all you wanted when you were sixteen, wasn't it? Women, about the age of thirty! I mean, that wasn't done in Liverpool, was it?![25]

Stories similar to this one and told as epic tales of a man's life were always commonplace in fo'c'sles and messrooms and are still told today where a voyage has taken a crew to Bangkok or wherever is the latest seaman's sensual paradise. Real or imagined, embroidered or knitted plain, 'heroic' drinking exploits and sexual 'conquests' were a critical part of a sailor's credentials and gave him the reputation of being a 'real man'.

The opportunities open to a young male to prove himself a man were not confined to the measures of drink and sex. Greater stature could be acquired through a reputation for adventurousness – such as deserting a ship abroad and working ashore or spirited independence in resisting a tyrannical chief engineer or Mate – both of which behaviours were common enough among Liverpool seamen. Seamen were itinerants on a global scale and desertion from larger ocean-going ships was extremely common. It attracted little comment in the immediate post-war years and was far from unknown in ships calling at Australasian ports in the 1960s. Occasional collections of statistics suggest that desertions, most of them in North America and Australasia, ran at a rate of approximately 10,000 a year from British ships in the period 1850–1910. In 1908 alone 23,311 deserted from ships abroad, 11,000 of them in the USA and Canada.[26] A few years later, in 1917, Britons accounted for more than half the membership of the American Seamen's Union and 75 per cent of the union's membership in the Atlantic trade.[27]

Desertion, or 'backing out' as it was known in Liverpool, was especially common amongst Liverpool seamen in the Atlantic ports of the USA and Canada. Bill Donaghy's career after deserting from an Elder Dempster ship in Montreal in 1928 was not untypical. He worked first on a ship trading to the Great Lakes, and when the Lakes froze over in winter he attempted to cross the border into the USA. Caught by immigration officers he was sent back to Montreal where he found another ship which was 'manned by people like me, deserters from British and other European ships'. This job lasted a few months and he then got a job on a farm – which also lasted just a few months. It was then into a factory job and yet another unsuccessful attempt at crossing the US border. On his release he got a ship and went to Australia and New Zealand and then called at New York on the voyage

home. There he met an old shipmate who had deserted
with him in Montreal but who had successfully got
across the border:

> Francie Cowan took me up to his house in Brooklyn
> and then we went on the town having a bloody great
> time, dancing with girls and everything. I thought:
> 'This is the life for me, I'm not going back to that ship.' I
> hadn't intended backing out of her and so I had to leave
> all my clothes and money in the ship.[28]

By then it was 1929 and a succession of jobs suitable
for an illegal immigrant followed – as did a marriage to
the daughter of Irish immigrants. In 1933, and now
with two children, jobs were impossible so he and his
family applied for voluntary deportation. On the
parish for fifteen months on his return, he eventually
got a job, through his uncle, as a ship-repairer with
Harland and Wolff's. This story is, of course, unique
in its detail. But many other stories – and of more
recent periods – can still be heard. Their social
function was much less to enhance the reputation of
the individual and much more to add to and improve
the image that dockland people had of themselves. The
same applied to the stories of men who stood up for
themselves and their shipmates while aboard ship.

Nineteenth-century Liverpool seamen had a reputation as being robust characters and shipmasters
were not normally flattering. A choleric American
master talking of the men on the fast sailing packets
on the North Atlantic run in the 1840s said they were
usually Liverpool-Irishmen who were: '... tough,
roustabout sailormen and difficult to handle, so that it
was sometimes a toss-up whether they or the captain
and officers would have charge of the ship ...'[29]

A British master, writing of Liverpool and its
seamen in the 1890s, said:

It has a good name, so far as ports go, though its
seamen are reputed to be responsible for more than
half the misdeeds and mysterious happenings on board
ship. When something goes wrong, or some wrong is
done and none comes forward to admit culpability,
then, 'it was the Liverpool feller wot done it.'[30]

Joseph Conrad, however, who did not ordinarily speak
well of fo'c'sle hands, said of one ship manned from
Liverpool: 'That crew of Liverpool hard cases had in
them the right stuff. It's my experience they always
have.'[31]

The early reputation of Liverpool seamen was
earned in sailing ships, and the advent of steam served
only to amplify it. The following newspaper report of a
prosecution brought against ship's firemen in 1901
revealed nothing remarkable to the seafaring and
shipowning community:

At the Liverpool City Police Court ... fourteen firemen
from the *Bohemian* were summoned for having ...
wilfully disobeyed the lawful commands of the chief
engineer. It was stated that when the ship was off
Holyhead ... nine of the men were ordered to turn out
and clean the engineroom. They positively refused to
obey the order, saying that they had had too much to do
during the voyage. Later in the day the other firemen
were ordered by the chief engineer to do the work, as
the ship was going into port, and they also refused. All
the men were logged [fined, T.L.] for disobedience.
Defendants were each sent to goal for 14 days without
the option of a fine.[32]

Another classic case of independent-mindedness
came to the attention of the same court in January
1943. The *Journal of Commerce* reported:

Because he disliked the master's attitude, Albert
Moore, twenty-year-old ship's fireman of Liverpool,
walked off the ship and went home. Accused at

Liverpool Police Court, yesterday, of deserting his ship, Moore said, 'When I went to the captain and asked him for my sub, he picked up his log-book [thereby implying disciplinary action, T.L.] and said, "What is your name?" I did not like his attitude, so I picked up my gear and left the ship.'

This report notes that Moore had been torpedoed in his previous ship and adrift in a boat for four days. He was fined £2.[33] In December of the same year three Liverpool firemen appeared in court in Birkenhead, accused of stealing ship's stores while in port in Nigeria. The prosecutor said: 'If the ship had been in Nigeria much longer, by the way things were going, certain members of the crew would have sold the ship herself.' Stolen goods were said to include an awning, hawsers and the wire used for hauling ashes from the engineroom; one night 'drums of paint were pushed through a porthole in the firemen's quarters into a waiting canoe ...' They were fined £8 each.[34] In every period there were similar cases to these. If they did not all get as far as magistrates' courts they certainly got into the ship's official log.

Forms of trading just as illegitimate – but more socially acceptable – were undertaken by seamen and were a normal feature of Liverpool dockland life. Their very normality and pervasiveness underlined, once again, the separateness of this society. Michael O'Mahoney, describing Park Lane as a cosmopolitan street in the 1920s, comments on '... a shop window which clamours "Parrots wanted"!'[35] Parrots were still wanted in this district in the 1950s, for it was close to the berth used by the Booth Line ships, home from the Amazon and with crew members having parrots to sell. Pet shop owners and dealers came from all over South Lancashire to meet seamen in the Lord de Tabley on Park Lane. Amongst the crew

were more serious traders, and of those the acknowl-
edged specialist was Barney Lafferty, nicknamed the
Animal Man. Entered on the ships' articles as able
seaman, and then lamp-trimmer and finally bosun,
Barney Lafferty was also a professional dealer. On his
first trip on the old passenger ship *Hilary* he
discovered that:

> ... the game there was parrots and monkeys. The
> monkeys were wonderful things, the woolly monkeys.
> They were very valuable – at present day prices you're
> talking something like £500. They're beautiful to look
> at and very placid, I've never known them to bite. Up
> the Amazon you could buy a parrot for £1 and you got
> £10 here for it; a woolly monkey would be £4 and you
> could get £20 and upwards depending on the quality.
> Some of mine went as far as Chester Zoo. There was
> also a store in the town where you could sell them. The
> owner was very good to do business with, he never took
> you for a ride. I sold a lot to him. I also sold woolly
> monkeys to Southport Zoo. Once you got to know them
> that was it – the owner at Southport would often come
> to the house with his van. You couldn't just go to
> Chester Zoo but some of the stuff this feller in town
> used to buy went to Chester Zoo.
>   I didn't only bring monkeys. I brought everything
> that walked or flew. Once, I had a thing like a huge rat
> in the house. I took this rat to the shop and some people
> from the zoo came to see it. They said they'd have it but
> didn't know how to take it. I told them to just pick it up.
> They said they wouldn't pick up anything like that –
> they said they lived on the roots of trees and they could
> lock their teeth around things. They said that if they
> locked their teeth into you they'd take the flesh as well
> and you'd be lucky if they left the bones. I told them it
> had been sleeping with me. This one was very tame and
> it used to follow me from the messroom into my cabin,
> just like a dog. It would go at the foot of my bunk and it
> had a habit of sucking my toes. The bloke from the zoo
> said, 'Good God, it's a wonder you've got any toes left.'
> It shook me a bit.[36]

Trading businesses were extremely common amongst seamen after the Second World War. They were all illicit – but the rewards were high. Nylons were smuggled in from the USA. There was a big trade in bicycle tubes and tyres to Holland and in the nail trade down to Las Palmas. Barney Lafferty reckons the profit margins were between 200 and 300 per cent. 'Each country was short of something,' says Barney, 'and it didn't take long for jolly Jacks to find out what was in demand. It kept men in certain ships.'[37] Compared with the prevailing wage rates the sums of money made on the side were often very substantial, but it was rare to the point of being almost unknown for the money to be accumulated. It was spent on big presents for wives, children and other members of the family. The rest might go on gambling, clothes, booze and women while away on voyage.

Serious gambling aboard ship was confined mainly to the passenger ships on the North Atlantic and to the cruise ships sailing for a season out of New York. Cooks and stewards could sometimes earn very substantial tips and once they had got them the gambling started. Fred Gregory, who first went to sea in 1936 as an officers' boy on the Canadian Pacific liner *Duchess of Bedford* says:

> ... they'd throw a couple of blankets on the deck and throw dice. There'd be 150 or 200 men all grouped round the men throwing the dice. This was on docking night in Montreal or Liverpool because they'd either had their tips off the passengers or were paid off. There might be a pot of $50 or $100 that they'd be throwing for, and this was before the war. On these passenger ships there was always gambling, always card games, all the time. It's part of a seaman's life really.[38]

Far more significant than the gambling on the passenger ships on the North Atlantic was the regular contact young seamen had with American habits and customs. Even before the First World War Americans were envied as being modern and stylish, and this was doubly true in Liverpool where working-class men could have direct contact with the USA. At the level of dress this was immediately obvious, for American fashions were copied by Liverpool tailors from clothes bought by seamen on the Eastern seaboard of the USA.[39] In the 1920s and 1930s broad-brimmed hats were favoured by Liverpool working-class politicoes who were keen to be associated with American radicalism.

After the Second World War the US influence was even greater, and not for nothing did many of the young seamen going there become known locally as 'Cunard Yanks'. They absorbed the democratic style of public manners they found in their contacts with East Coast working Americans; they adapted their vocabularies to include American idioms; they bought American shirts and ties ... and recordings of American popular music long before it was released in the UK. For the vast bulk of the British population, American culture was transmitted through the cinema, but in Liverpool's docklands there was a long-standing direct link through the seamen who regularly travelled there and through the seamen who had deserted, worked ashore on the waterfront in New York or Boston and then taken jobs on American ships which traded back to Liverpool.

It is hard to exaggerate the influence of seamen in Liverpool life. All those stories – of gambling and illicit trading, of womanising and drinking in foreign ports, of being on the beach in the USA and Australia, of irreverence to chiefs and skippers – produced an image and an ideal of a highly desirable freewheeling life of adventure and independence. Of course the *practice* contained only the merest fraction of the colourful promise – but then the truth of the matter was utterly irrelevant. What mattered was that the *message* of the stories represented an account of 'the sort of people we are'. The meaning of the stories was not in any actual events described but in the contribution every 'event' made to an overall picture of a 'man's life'. This picture became a mirror and the people of dockland could then look at it and see themselves with pride. While the self-image was constructed out of male conceptions and male experiences, the process of translation of the image into everyday attitudes and behaviour left male and female Liverpudlians indistinguishable: both being equally assertive and defiant in their prideful refusal to bend the knee to anyone. The fact that women were as defiant and assertive as men did not mean, however, that women merely echoed men's rhetoric. The role of women in the management of the household economy was formidable and we have caught glimpses of this in several examples. Women were infinitely more 'street-wise' than men in the ways of survival and this experience gave them their own deep reservoirs of independence.

The traditions and practices of seafarers, diffused through the dockland districts over many generations and mixed with the experiences of family, neighbour-hood and other casual occupations undoubtedly gave *all* citizens of the other Liverpool a common identity. But if all these citizens drew on this identity, they were, nonetheless, *dis*united. The lines of cleavage are well known: religion and ethnicity.

In the 1980s the religious divisions have dis-appeared, even though the Orange Lodges still march on 12 July with their banners and uniformed bands. There is no longer any sense of riotous carnival as in

the 1920s and 1930s when Catholics would turn out to
wait for the Lodges' return after an outing to
Southport. Bill Hudson, then a policeman, was often
detailed to escort the bands and he says:

> It was really funny sometimes. You'd see all the girls
> up on St George's plateau and when the Orange Lodge
> people came out they'd lift up their skirts and show all
> their green knickers.[40]

This was the more innocuous part, but even when it
got rougher the confrontatons of 12 July seem to have
been decidedly ritualistic. Here Frank Baker describes
a typical course of events in the South End of the city
in the 1930s:

> In those days there'd be a boy or girl dressed up as
> William of Orange and stuck up on top of a horse with a
> big sword in his hand. Now and again he might stand
> up in his stirrups and wave his sword around and
> everybody would be shouting, 'Aye, aye, Billy was a
> hero!' Once the march got into Catholic areas things
> would be different. The police would put barriers across
> certain streets but there were still the Catholics living
> in the houses on either side of the street. It was nothing
> for bags of pepper to be thrown – or even worse! ... We
> used to walk with the Lodge and on the corner of Upper
> Parliament Street, by the Anglican Cathedral, any-
> thing could happen. If you didn't watch out you could
> get crowned, broken bottles were thrown. Then the
> men in the ranks carried real swords – and if it came to
> a scuffle they'd use them an' all.[41]

Jimmy Halsall, living in the same area, said:

> In the part of Beaufort Street that we lived in there
> were only three Protestant families and every 12 July
> their windows would go in, every one of them. They
> even set fire to a house one time. These were cellar

houses and the cellars were never used and one time a mattress was put in and set alight.

But as he said, it was only on 12 July:

> At other times you'd be playing with Catholic kids. I used to go to the boxing club at St Malachy's church and when I was older in the Young Men's Society playing billiards. There used to be twopenny hops at the Irish League in Mill Street. I was a Protestant but that didn't stop me going.[42]

Jimmy Halsall, however, lived in a street where Protestant and Catholic families overlapped and this was not common, except where Protestant and Catholic streets met to form a frontier. Whole blocks of streets, whole areas were clearly recognised as either Catholic or Protestant until the clearances of the 1950s and 1960s tore them down. At the turn of the century the lines of religious adherence were clearly drawn and could easily be identified in the statistics of school attendance. In 1900 in the Dingle 89 per cent of children attended either council or Church of England schools, the remaining 11 per cent going to Catholic schools. In South Scotland the order, if not the magnitude, was reversed: 70 per cent went to Catholic schools and 30 per cent to council or Church of England schools.

Especially for the Catholics, the parish organisation was all pervasive and the priest apparently all powerful. Recalling his early teenage years in the late 1940s, living in Hornby Street tenements which were in the very heart of Catholic Liverpool, Gerry Caughey said:

> The priest was a frightening figure, an avenging angel and you really feared him. With the cops you could run away and you could even escape from the Sisters at

school – but you couldn't get the better of the priest. You see, your parents and everyone else was on his side. Against anyone from outside you had allies, but against the priest you had none.[43]

The power of the Catholic parishes did not only lie with the priests. Given powerful anti-Irish sentiments and a long history of persecution, the Catholic Church and its adherents acted as though beleaguered. These historical factors, taken together with the normal authoritarianism of the church, made Catholic parishes utterly unlike their Anglican equivalents in the extent to which they attempted to control their parishioners. The most obvious control was exercised through the monopolisation of the rituals of the calendar of life and especially the sacraments of death. Just as important were the networks or organisations and associations for children, youth, men and women. All of these provided some certainty, some framework, some sources of solidarity in a hostile environment of uncertain income and discriminatory employers.

Protestantism was rarely the equal and opposite of Catholicism – partly because Protestantism was no less schismatic in docklands than it was anywhere else. In general, Protestantism was defined more in terms of attitudes to the Irish and to Catholics than with reference to a denominational membership. Where there were positive affiliations, Protestantism might mean association with an Anglican church with a militantly low-church incumbent or membership of a wholly independent and localised evangelical organisation, such as the Sailors' Chapel in the Dingle which had Orange links. Associated with Protestant churches there was as wide a range of clubs and other bodies as there was in Catholic parishes but allegiances were scattered, sometimes competitive and nearly always lacking the Catholic strengths of centralised control and discipline. But Protestantism at its most highly organised could be the equal of Catholicism. In 1921 the Protestant Reformers Memorial Church – the bastion of Liverpool Protestantism – had an extraordinary range of activities:

> There are fourteen organisations connected with the Church, and on Sunday afternoon every place is fully occupied, and a gathering of about 700 men meet in the Church. The Sunday School, comprising 800 scholars, is crowded out, also a primary class in a small room and two women's classes. During the week Christian Endeavour Societies meet, also Debating and Literary Societies. We have also an Economics Study Class to counteract the extreme element of the Labour Party. This class holds open-air meetings almost every night throughout the city and district. We are not in a position to pay an assistant, all of the work being carried on by a band of loyal workers, bearing all their own out-of-pocket expenses.[44]

This case, however, was unique in its extensiveness and other organisations might depend on patronage from a local employer to provide them with new recruits. Frank Baker, for example, got his first permanent job at Wilson's flour mill in the Dingle through his membership of the Beresford Street Mission which was used by F.C. Wilson as a source of reliable labour:

> At Beresford Street on the Sunday morning there would be as many as 400 kids and Mr Kelly, an iron-moulder by trade, who ran the place had good backing from F.C. Wilson. Every year at the Beresford Street Mission prize-giving, Mr Wilson and his wife used to come and give out the prizes. All the little boys had to go to the platform and salute Mrs Wilson and all

the little girls had to go and bow to Mr Wilson to get their prizes.[45]

Presumably Bibby's, in the North End, used similar methods, for on leaving school in the 1930s Barney Lafferty remembered being told by his headmaster not to apply for jobs there because they did not take on Catholics. Segregation in the workplace on the grounds of religious affiliation was common. No chief engineer of a coalburning ship would knowingly engage both Catholic and Protestant firemen, and foremen on the docks were often notorious for their religious preferences. Bill Downey remembers his father, a Harrison's foreman in the 1930s:

> ... shouting down the hatch to a bloke who was working in a green shirt, 'If that shirt's not changed at dinnertime, you won't be working.' That was just because he had a green shirt on. I used to say to him when I was older how wrong he was. I remember when television first came on and he'd say, 'Look, there's another Irish face.'[46]

Just as Catholics and Protestants had their city quarters, so too did the Chinese, the West Africans and handfuls of Filipinos, Malays, Somalis, Indians and West Indians. Also in that district, close to the Sailors' Home and the Shipping Office, were boarding houses specialising in providing lodging for Swedes, Norwegians, Germans and Spaniards who arrived in Liverpool as members of ships' crews. 40 per cent of able seamen who signed on in Liverpool for voyages in sailing ships in 1891 were foreigners, mainly Germans and Scandinavians but including smaller numbers of French, Dutch, Belgians, Italians and North Americans. By far the greatest number of Europeans, temporarily or permanently resident, were Norwegians and Swedes, and both nationalities had their own churches. At the turn of the century there was some pride in the cosmopolitan nature of the city. Not only did it offer further proof of the city's international stature, but it also provided another opportunity to boast. According to Ramsay Muir:

> There is no city in the world, not even London itself, in which so many foreign governments find it necessary to maintain consular offices for the safeguarding of the interests of their exiled subjects.[47]

Black seamen were extremely common on sailing ships and most of them were from one of the Caribbean islands or from the USA. Most often they were employed as cooks, sometimes as stewards and not infrequently as able seamen. The *normal* sailing ship's fo'c'sle was amazingly polyglot. When the *Baroda*, for example, sailed from Liverpool for Calcutta in July 1880, she had a Chinese cook, three West Indian ABs, one Norwegian, one Dane, two Germans, two Welshmen, three Londoners, two from Sussex and one from Bristol.[48] This kind of melting pot was extremely common and often the result of ships losing men abroad through sickness or desertion, and then engaging replacements – but the replacements themselves had often been deposited by a series of previous ships. When the Liverpool ship *Coronet* replaced the largely British crew who had deserted in Canada in 1880, she signed on as replacements in St John six West Indians, two Canadians and three Americans.[49]

Foreign seamen were not so often employed on steamships – comprising only 13 per cent of engagements in Liverpool in 1901 – although a local

ship might well engage in Antwerp a crew of
Estonians, Finns and Belgians and then discharge
them all in Liverpool at the end of the voyage. If some
would have made their way back to Antwerp, the more
usual practice would be to spend a few days in
Liverpool and then find another ship or wait for the
ship they had just left to sign on again. In the case of
the latter, the period elapsed might be two weeks and
for that period the crew would become local residents.
It was for such people, rather than for local seamen,
that sailortown catered. 'Every sailorman knows Lime
Street', said Pat O'Mara,

> and certainly every foreigner knows Italian 'Jew'
> Grossi's Trocadero, the English counterpart of the
> Continental boozer-bordello, in the basement of the
> Hotel St George. The big Sailors' Outfitters store over
> to the left in Paradise Street is also owned by Mr
> Grossi. Here sailormen took their advance notes and
> had them exchanged 75 per cent in merchandise, 25
> per cent cash – this last usually finding its way back to
> Grossi via his Trocadero.[50]

Foreign seamen contributed to the cosmopolitan
nature of Liverpool because they formed a constant, if
shifting, presence. Of these seamen, some settled and
their descendants' names are liberally scattered
through the pages of the telephone directory. Other
transient seamen – Indians, for example – never
settled. Their conditions of employment, after racial
incidents in London early in the nineteenth century,
required them to be repatriated at the ship's expense.
But in Liverpool they were still a familiar sight to the
people of dockland as they passed through the streets
on their way to Paddy's Market which sold second-
hand goods. For Peter Breen, living in the South End,
it was all part of the local atmosphere:

I remember the Coolies coming up and going back to
the Harrison boats. They always used to walk one
behind the other in single file – the same as the police
used to do at that particular time. I've seen the Coolies
coming back from Paddy's Market in Scotland Road
with bowler hats piled up on their heads, then maybe
another would be carrying a gramophone with a big
horn. That was a sight worth seeing.[51]

Liverpool folklore sometimes has it that the city's
black population is descended from slaves landed in
the city. There is no reason to believe this. Slaves
transported on Liverpool ships were not brought to
Britain, although some wealthy households with
plantation connections in the West Indies did have
small numbers of black servants. Any other black
residents, temporary or permanent, would have come
as seamen and been shipped as replacements for dead
or diseased European seamen in West Africa, the West
Indies or the USA. Black seamen from these regions
became a more common sight in Liverpool as the
nineteenth century progressed, and were not especially strange in the 1830s. Herman Melville remarked:

In Liverpool indeed the negro steps with a prouder
pace, and lifts his head like a man; for here, no such
exaggerated feeling exists in respect to him, as in
America. Three or four times I encountered our black
steward, dressed very handsomely, and walking arm in
arm with a good-looking English woman. In New York,
such a couple would have been mobbed in three
minutes; and the steward would have been lucky to
have escaped with whole limbs. Owing to the friendly
reception extended to them, and the unwonted
immunities they enjoy in Liverpool, the black cooks
and stewards of American ships are very much
attached to the place and like to make voyages to it.[52]

The earliest and largest group of non-Europeans to
form a settlement were almost certainly Kru (or Kroo)

men from the Liberian coast who were highly regarded
as seamen. One of the earliest references, from 1801,
describes 'Kroos or Kroomen' as

> ... a very industrious people [who] frequently engage
> themselves to European vessels upon the coast,
> continuing aboard several months, and acting in the
> capacity of sailors and traders, in both which situations
> they show much intelligence and activity.[53]

From working with ships on the coast it was a short
step to returning to the UK with the ship – or going in
the other direction, to India, as a stoker on a ship of the
Royal Navy.[54] By the 1870s Krumen formed a regularly
replenished colony in Liverpool when it became a
normal practice for Elder Dempster ships to engage
them in Freetown, Sierra Leone. At that time they
were shipped as ABs, cooks and stewards or as
firemen, lived in the same quarters as European
seamen and were paid the same wages. Shipboard
segregation began in the 1890s when they had their
own quarters, worked only as firemen and received
lower wages than Europeans.[55]

In character, Krumen were well suited to Liverpool
for they too had a reputation for being hard-working
but independent-minded. Attempts at various times to
recruit Kru for indentured labour in the West Indies
were unsuccessful and when working as navvies on the
Panama Canal they went on strike, demanding to be
repatriated after deaths among them from malnu-
trition diseases.[56] David Livingstone also experienced
difficulty when in 1858 he recruited twelve Krumen to
man the launch for his Zambezi expedition. This went
well enough but they later refused to work as his
bearers when on land and were sent back to Freetown
on a naval ship.[57]

Many black Liverpudlians are descendants, in the male line, of Kru seamen who by the 1890s no longer stayed in boarding houses, having established their own households. According to Pat O'Mara, they were highly regarded as husbands by white women:

> Not only were [they] ... accepted by white women as equals; many times they were regarded as the white man's superior. The main reason, of course, was economic – they made better *pater familiae*.[58]

Pat O'Mara was writing of the 1900s, by which time the name 'Kru' had become reduced in meaning to the point where it was used by white shipowners and ships' officers to mean any black African seaman. The great majority of seamen engaged in West Africa were still Krumen, although by then most were permanently resident in Freetown where they were regularly hired to take European ships around the West African ports, acting as a mobile stevedoring force. Those who were hired as seamen were increasingly supplemented by Nigerians signed on in Calabar and Lagos, and men from Cape Coast, in what is now Ghana – many of these, too, became Liverpool residents.

Manpower shortages in the UK in both world wars led to increases in the numbers of men recruited to be seafarers from many other corners of the empire. It was at this time that Cardiff and South Shields acquired their Arabic-speaking populations – usually known as 'Somali' because most came from regions around the Gulf of Aden. Smaller numbers of 'Somali' based themselves in Liverpool for they were mainly employed by the tramp companies of the Bristol Channel and the North-East coast. Small numbers of West Indians had lived in Liverpool for as long as ships had traded to the islands, but most of them were as

transient as all other seafarers until substantial
recruitments of seamen in Barbados and Trinidad
during the Second World War. In the 1950s and early
1960s the area in which Africans, West Indians and
Arabic-speaking people lived was enlivened by the
black American servicemen from the Burtonwood
airbase who visited for their social life. By this time,
too, the 'colour-bar' on American merchant ships was
easing off and seamen from visiting US ships made
Liverpool 8 their home while in port.

In adjacent streets, but retaining their separate
identity, were the Chinese. Ships had picked up
Chinese in ones and twos as replacement crew long
before the middle of the nineteenth century, but
Chinese were not seen in any number until Alfred
Holt, looking for economies, began recruiting Chinese
seamen in 1892–93. The numbers who became
permanently resident were very small but in 1906 a
racist panic had been fomented by the *Liverpool
Courier* and this then led to a city council-sponsored
Commission of Inquiry. The resultant report gestured
to racial sentiment but was generally dismissive of
allegations about opium and gambling dens and other
'decadent' activities tacitly believed to be sapping the
vitality of the 'imperial race'.

The Chinese population, counted in several hundreds in 1906, had probably doubled by 1939. It was
war, once again, that quickly produced a very large
increase. Chinese seamen were normally recruited in
Hong Kong, Singapore and Shanghai, but soon after
the entry of Japan into the war these ports were closed
and ships which had once changed crews there were
now obliged to change them in UK ports. Although
London's Chinese community was at least as old as
Liverpool's, it was Liverpool that became the temporary place of residence for thousands of Chinese

seafarers. Many of them stayed after the war to help form what soon became Europe's largest Chinese community. This community was then supplemented in the 1950s and 1960s with migrants who came direct from Hong Kong. In the 1960s the Chinese presence in Liverpool was far more pronounced than that of any other group, largely through their dominance of all but the most expensive end of the restaurant trade.[59]

Always excepting the internal migrations of Irish, Welsh and Scottish, the largest migrant group before the Chinese came were Jewish refugees from pogroms in Poland and Russia in the 1890s and 1900s. Jewish people did not settle in docklands in any number. There was already an area of previous Jewish settlement which lay close to the city but beyond the dockland belt. This district was the only artisan-workshop quarter of the city and the last remnants of what was once a busy district for the furnishing and tailoring trades still remain. The Jews were the only one of the ethnically distinct migrant groups that became part of the respectable working class. Economic adjustment was for them a fairly easy matter, having a command of European artisanal and linguistic skills. With the exception of the Jews who accomplished the difficult task of remaining culturally separate but economically assimilated, the ethnic minorities were confined to their quarters of the city in docklands, and except for the Chinese, were all but invisible to the rest of the population. This was largely because they were far more continuously seafarers than the rest of the population. Discriminatory practices kept them out of almost all port employments except seafaring – and even on ships it was hard for black seafarers to get jobs in many of the liner companies until the acute labour shortages of the 1960s. Separateness was forced upon the black population rather than voluntarily entered into. The mushroom growth of ethnically related clubs – the Somali, the Sierra Leone, the Ghana, the Yoruba, the Ibo, the Gambia – developed in response to rebuffs elsewhere.

Liverpool docklands certainly had an extremely varied population, but only those of European origin were wholly assimilated and accepted. The others experienced enforced segregation in jobs and in housing even though intermarriage was the norm until the arrival, after the Second World War, of African, West Indian and Chinese women. Nevertheless, the descendants of West African, Chinese and West Indian men are as unmistakeably Liverpudlian as white Catholics and Protestants. Despite the discriminations and the prejudices, the essential experiences of living in the other Liverpool has made them as naturally democratic as their white neighbours.

Notes

1 Nathaniel Hawthorne, *The English Notebooks*, New York 1941, p.50.
2 Capt. Hardy (pseudonym), Ocean Steamship Co., in an interview with the author, 27 July 1983.
3 This figure is derived from the 1901 Census by aggregating the following ward populations: Brunswick, Great George, Exchange, North Scotland, St Peters, South Scotland, Vauxhall, Sandhills, plus 50 per cent of the population of Dingle and Kirkdale and 25 per cent of that of Netherfield, St Domingo, Everton and Princes Park wards.
4 Ramsay Muir, *A History of Liverpool*, Liverpool 1907, p.306.
5 F.J. Hanham, *Report of an Enquiry into Casual Labour on Merseyside*, London 1930, pp.2 and 9.
6 Albert Rose, Foreman shipwright, Mersey Dock and Harbour Company in an interview with the author, 29 June 1978.
7 P.J. Waller, *Democracy and Sectarianism*, Liverpool 1981, p.83.
8 Quoted in ibid., p.84.
9 *Liverpool Courier*, 14 September 1906.

10 *Proceedings of Council*, 1905, p.44; 1912, p.279.
11 Details of Burlington Street from *Gore's Directory*, 1909 and electoral register, South Scotland Ward, 1901–2.
12 *Liverpool Review*, 8 July 1899.
13 R. Williams, for the Liverpool Economics and Statistical Society, *The First Year's Working of the Liverpool Docks Scheme*, Liverpool 1914.
14 Quoted in *Liverpool Courier*, 24 January 1911.
15 Bob Edwards, registered dock labourer, Mersey Dock and Harbour Company, in an interview with the author, 12 April 1978.
16 John Dooligan, ship's cook, in an interview with the author 14 September 1983.
17 Tony Santamera, Liverpool branch secretary, National Union of Seamen, in an interview with the author, 31 October 1983.
18 C. Caradog Jones, *The Social Survey of Merseyside*, Vol. II, Liverpool 1934, p.44.
19 J.M.M. Hill, *The Seafaring Career*, London 1972, Appendix I.
20 *Census*, 1851; *Committee of Inquiry into Shipping*, Cmnd. 4337, 1970, Table 13.2, p.232.
21 Joseph McKeown, *Back Crack Boy*, London 1980 p.109.
22 John Cornelius, *Liverpool 8*, London 1982, pp.13–4.
23 Hill, op.cit., p.61.
24 Herman Melville, *Redburn*, Harmondsworth 1977, p.263.
25 Quoted in T. Lane, *Grey Dawn Breaking*, Manchester 1986, p.140.
26 *Return Respecting the Number of Desertions from British Ships*, Cmnd. 4803, 1909, pp.10–19.
27 A.H. Jenks, *Continuity of Employment in the Merchant Navy*, unpublished M.A. thesis, University of Liverpool, 1953, p.26.
28 Bill Donaghy, late secretary, Liverpool Pensioners Trade Union, in interviews with the author, March and April, 1978.
29 A.H. Clark, *The Clipper Ship Era, 1843–1869*, New York 1910, p.122.
30 J.W. Harris, *Days of Endeavour*, London 1932, p.228.
31 Joseph Conrad, *Youth*, Harmondsworth 1981, p.26.
32 Quoted in *Journal of Marine Engineers Association*, January 1901, p.21.
33 *Journal of Commerce*, 27 January 1943.
34 Ibid., 28 December 1943.
35 Michael O'Mahoney, *Liverpool Ways and Byeways*, Liverpool 1931, p.136.
36 Barney Lafferty, retired bosun, Ellerman Lines, in an interview with the author, November and December 1986.
37 Ibid.
38 Fred Gregory, retired chief steward, Canadian Pacific Steamships, in an interview with the author, August 1985.

39 See Pat O'Mara, *The Autobiography of a Liverpool Slummy*, London 1934, p.293.

40 Bill Hudson, retired police sergeant, in an interview with the author, 3 July 1978.

41 Frank Baker, retired mill-worker, in an interview with the author, 23 April 1978.

42 Jimmy Halsall, retired blacksmith, Mersey Dock and Harbour Company, in an interview with the author, 12 April 1978.

43 Gerry Caughey, Convenor, St Helens Unemployed Centre, in an interview with the author, January 1971.

44 Quoted in Waller, op.cit., p.286.

45 Frank Baker interview, loc. cit.

46 Bill Downey, retired docker, in an interview with the author, 6 April 1978.

47 Muir, op.cit., p.305.

48 Crew Lists of ship, *Baroda*, 1880, Liverpool Record Office.

49 Crew Lists of ship, *Coronet*, 1880, Liverpool Record Office.

50 O'Mara, op. cit., pp.8–9.

51 Peter Breen, retired joiner, in an interview with the author, May 1978.

52 Melville, op. cit., p.277.

53 T. Winterbottom, *An Account of the Native Africans in the Neighbourhood of Sierra Leone*, London 1801 (1969 edn), p.9.

54 *First Report from the Select Committee on Indian Territories*, Vol. XXVII, 1852–53, Evidence of Capt. Hall, RN, Q's: 232–33.

55 Crew Lists of: *Africa*, 29 March 1873 – 5 May 1881: *Burutu*, 28 June 1902 – 26 August 1912, Liverpool Record Office.

56 C. Fyfe, *A History of Sierra Leone*, Oxford 1962, p.547.

57 C.P. Groves, *Planting of Christianity in Africa*, Vol. II, 1954, p.178.

58 O'Mara, op. cit., pp.11–2.

59 See Maria Lin Davies, 'Chinese Liverpudlians', unpublished B.A. Dissertation (Economic History), University of Liverpool, 1986.

4 Boss Politics

Liverpool politics have never been less than puzzling and exasperating to outsiders and insiders alike. It was certainly a strange English city that could return an Irish Nationalist MP for one of its constituencies, from 1885 until 1929. It was no less strange for having a Protestant Party which even in 1971 had four councillors in the Town Hall.

In the nineteenth century Liverpool stayed almost continuously Tory when other cities were far more likely to be Liberal. In the twentieth century it was a city which remained Tory when others were becoming Labour. Sheffield, for example, was thirty years ahead of Liverpool in electing a Labour council; even London was twenty years ahead. When Labour eventually took

over the direction of the city administration, in 1955,
the Tories had enjoyed more than one hundred years
control of the city council.

No sooner had Labour started to win more elections
than it lost (having an overall majority on the council
for nine of the fifteen years between 1955 and 1970)
than a Liberal revival began, and in 1973 the Liberals
became the largest single party. This development,
once again, made Liverpool look decidedly odd, for in
none of the other large cities had the Liberals made
any major inroad into the Labour vote. Finally, and as
if to crown the city's political eccentricities, an
extremely well organised Trotskyist sect gained
control of the city council itself in 1983. This 'coup',
unparalleled in British politics, led to some predictably
adventurist practices which ended in defeat in the law
courts in 1987.

The apparent peculiarities of Liverpool politics are
easily translated into normality once set in the context
of the city's history and the character and composition
of its working-class population. This chapter is mainly
concerned with the politics of labour in Liverpool, for in
this city, as elsewhere in the UK and Western Europe,
the most significant political development of the
twentieth century has been the rise of labour and its
organisations. Inevitably, labour developed differently
in form and pace according to regional economic and
cultural variations and nowhere, perhaps, has this
been so evident as in Liverpool.

In the course of the 1960s Liverpool and its region
acquired a national reputation for being a centre of
trade union militancy. In that decade the view began
to take root, almost as much in the Labour Party as
among Conservatives, that trade union usurpation of
managerial authority in the workplace was latent

everywhere and, in places like Liverpool, often manifest. On the face of it, this is strange because Liverpool's earlier history of trade unionism and working-class political action had been backward and unreliable.

On those few occasions in the twentieth century when British governments have been genuinely, if mistakenly, anxious about working-class activity, they have looked at Clydeside and the coalfields of South Wales and the Scottish Lowlands. It is true that in the decade before the First World War, and again in 1981, incidents in Liverpool provoked unease at the Home Office – but these were matters of public order without any basis in organised politics or movements. Referring to riots in Liverpool in August 1911, the Home Secretary Winston Churchill said: 'You need not attach great importance to the rioting last night, it took place in an area where disorder is a chronic feature.'[1] The British Communist Party arrived at a similar conclusion in the 1930s – its organisers reckoned Liverpool to be an anarchic place where spontaneity and flamboyant gestures were preferred to the disciplines of tactical thinking and planned interventions. Liverpool was an organisers' graveyard.[2]

There is no evidence that the old families, or Liverpool's propertied classes in general, were ever especially alarmed about the political intentions and ambitions of Liverpool's working classes. In the metropolis the situation was quite different. In the second half of the nineteenth century the urban poor of London were being labelled as the 'volcanic masses', the 'dangerous classes', the people of 'the abyss' or the 'nether world'. The labels reflected the anxieties of the wealthy and others who thought they had something substantial to lose. Metropolitan fears quickened, especially after the London dock strike in 1889 when, for the very first time, the 'dangerous classes' began to look organised. A strike of similar dimensions in Liverpool in the following year did not seem to awaken comparable worries.

Among the elite of Liverpool there was a well developed awareness of the existence of another Liverpool. Shimmin consistently wrote of the other Liverpool as if it were a separate society with its own social practices and codes of behaviour. Even if this reportage was not widely read it must nevertheless have passed into the background knowledge of the classes who talked over dinner. This other world, however, was either an object of uneasy conscience or moral outrage, but not of fear. Nathaniel Hawthorne's observations on the matter were, as always, extremely interesting. Plainly not a member of the local elite, he was nevertheless acutely conscious of the elite's manners and attitudes. If there had been any anxiety among them toward the urban poor he would surely have picked it up. And yet his description of a visit to a poor quarter of the city paints it as 'picturesque' and the people passive:

> Almost every day, I take walks about Liverpool; preferring the darker and dingier streets, inhabited by the poorer classes. The scenes there are very picturesque in their way; at every two or three steps, a gin shop ... women nursing their babies at dirty bosoms; men haggard, drunken, care-worn, hopeless, but with a kind of patience, as if all this were the rule of their life.[3]

Thirty years later Hugh Farrie was writing in the *Liverpool Daily Post* of the enormous gulf between wealth and poverty but, here again, there is no sense of threat:

[A district off Scotland Road] is as dirty, tumble-down,
and as unhealthy as any portion of squalid Liverpool,
and it lies within a stone's-throw of prosperous
money-making Liverpool – the Liverpool of clubs, of
cafes, of banks, of commercial places. Walk along Dale
Street as the sun glistens on the shop windows,
throwing the shadow of the lofty spire of the Municipal
Offices like the pointer of a huge sundial across the
street; as gossiping politicians lounge on the steps of
the Reform Club and the Conservative Club; as
carriages rattle along, conveying wealthy merchants
from splendid offices to suburban halls; you find traces
wherever your eye turns of wealth and ambiton ... of
busy, happy men, all bent upon winning some prize in
the world, and you might easily imagine that no dark
shade of squalor rested upon the broad face of
Liverpool. Yet walk a few paces from this bright and
cheering scene, and you will find gathered upon the
very edge of it a deep fringe of suffering, helpless,
hopeless poverty, all the more distressing in that it is
so near a region of hope, of comfort, and of activity.[4]

This is a call to conscience. Poverty is 'suffering'; it is
'helpless', 'hopeless', 'distressing' – but not alarming or
intimidating. During the decade or so before the First
World War middle- and upper-class awareness of
urban poverty had been substantially sharpened. The
abysmal state of health of thousands of volunteers to
fight in the Boer War led to anxieties about the
physical condition of the 'imperial race'. Booth and
Rowntree had produced the first scientific poverty
surveys and the Royal Commission on the Poor Laws
had amassed a mountain of evidence. In Liverpool
interest focused on casual labour and its consequences
and there were only minor political undertones in the
introduction to a pamphlet *How the Casual Labourer
Lives* published in 1909:

Everything about the system of employment seems to
foster the formation of bad habits and nothing to

encourage the formation of good ones. The alternations
of hard work and idleness disincline the men to steady
exertion. The uncertainty of earnings encourages
concealment from the wife and by accustoming the
family to existence at the standard of bad weeks sets
the surplus of good ones free for self-indulgence ... The
consciousness that no certificate of character will be
asked for, and that prolonged absence from the dock on
a drinking bout will not perceptibly lessen the chance
of employment on reappearance, removes all the
natural checks and penalties which in other professions do so much to keep the average man straight. The
haphazard method of selection and the dependence of
the men upon the goodwill of the foremen encourages
petty corruption and tyranny and lowers the tone and
self-respect of the employed.[5]

Even after the general transport strike in 1911 there
was no indication that Liverpool's ruling classes were
drenched in anxiety. A rolling strike which embraced
seamen, dockers, carters, railwaymen and tram-
waymen brought troops into the city and turned
suburban parks into armed encampments – but there
was no suggestion of panic amongst the old families.

The moral panic which seemed to grip metropolitan
observers of developments amongst the working
classes was simply absent in Liverpool. Of course there
were fears about the longer-run implications of some of
the programmes of sections of the workers'
movements, and these were naturally voiced – but
none of the people living in the big houses seemed to be
proclaiming the imminent end of 'the world as we know
it'. The difference in attitude and outlook between the
metropolitan and the Liverpool ruling classes was a
function of the social and political networks that each
was tied into. Where the metropolitans were rootless
in the sense of not being anchored and enmeshed in
specifically local institutions, the Liverpool ruling

classes had their connections with either the Tory or
Liberal parties as well as other affiliations which kept
them well informed of what was happening in the city.
Each party had its connections with other sections of
the population, especially the other Liverpool of the
dockland districts. The Tories, with the Working Men's
Conservative Association (Catholics excluded from
membership) reached into Protestant docklands and
the Liberals, through their electoral pacts with the
Irish Nationalists, reached into Catholic docklands.
The old families' connections with philanthropic
organisation also brought them some intelligence of
the other Liverpool.

The old families had themselves largely withdrawn
from direct participation in local politics long before
the end of the nineteenth century. This was partly
because their businesses, now national and international in scope, had outgrown local dependencies. It
was also a function of extensions of the franchise which
had eroded the power of wealthy individuals as
patrons and created the need for permanent party
organisations. The old families, having adopted much
of the style and education of the gentry, were
disdainful of the need to associate with their social
inferiors in electoral politics. Remarking on this,
Orchard claimed that the presence of people like John
Taggart, local secretary of the Gas and General
Labourers' Union, on the city council was '... used to
justify the refusal of well-educated, commercially
trained and competent gentlemen to attend where they
must meet such on equal social ground'.[6]

The withdrawal from local politics was not total.
There were a few family members or business
associates who enjoyed fixing and stitching and they
continued to be councillors or aldermen – and there

were a few others who were driven by their convictions. Behind the scenes, in the rooms of the political clubs – the Constitutional for the Tories, the Reform and Junior Reform for the Liberals – there remained great scope for influence. The wealthy contributed most of the money to maintain party organisations and expected, in return, to have some voice in the selection of candidates in elections.

By the 1930s the Liberals were finished as a political force and most of the old families who remained had become Tories. Among the Tories the writ of the Derbys still ran strong. In the 1930s, Sir Joseph Cleary, then a relatively young and unknighted Labour councillor, was privately approached by the Tories with a view to taking over the leadership of the Tory group on the city council: he was assured that the approach was being made with the knowledge and approval of Lord Derby.[7] The business community also retained a vestige of its old power through its control of the Castle Street ward. In the heart of the city's banking district, this ward with a population of 124 still returned three councillors (who were invariably unopposed) in 1951.

The twentieth-century descendants of the old families incurred few penalties for their personal absence from political office. The local middle class of shopkeepers, owners of small businesses, architects, accountants and solicitors who ran the Tory Party were too economically dependent upon the success of the port to be other than utterly reliable from the point of view of the elite. Tory councillors were from the 'real' middle class – they were generally people who employed small numbers of workers and who were in daily, face-to-face contact with them. If they were shopkeepers or other small traders then their customers were mainly the regularly employed

manual or white-collar working class. If they were
professionals they might have some contact with the
wealthier sections of the business community. These
two sections of the middle class were also typically
composed of people who were upwardly mobile and
therefore had family connections with the two main
sections of the respectable working class. These
organic links were extremely important. Even with the
limited franchise before universal male suffrage in
1918 the Tories could never get a majority without
substantial working-class support. With adult suffrage
finally secured in 1928, the importance for the Tories of
securing substantial working-class support increased
rather than diminished.

The respectable working class consisted of two
sections. There were the white-collar workers in
offices, banks and shops who by the turn of the century
were living in what were then the outer suburbs. And
there were the regularly employed and mainly skilled
manual workers who lived in the tidy terraced streets
adjacent to the city and docklands. The discussion here
will focus on the manual workers because it was within
their ranks that the real struggles for political
allegiance were conducted.

Among the regularly employed manual workers the
terms 'rough' and 'respectable' were widely used as a
means of maximising the social distance between
themselves and the under- and unemployed. Of course
the division was essentially a matter of income, but it
was usually expressed in terms of housing – as the
following letter to the *Liverpool Daily Post* in 1908 very
neatly shows:

> But will persons who can afford to pay 6s. a week, or
> even 5s., only consent to be packed with those paying
> 1s. or even 1s. 6d. for one room? One may be built for

the basket woman and the other for the artisan. When
the artisan knows his neighbour, will he be comfortable
and content? Unfortunately the working classes have
their bias, like the parson and the squire. The artisan
thinks himself a cut above the labourer, and the skilled
worker will walk around the man who only obtains a
casual job.[8]

This letter, dubiously signed 'A Workingman', was
published in the course of a debate in the city on the
provision of council housing, and the suggestion came
from some quarters that the council should provide
housing for all working people rather than only the
casually employed. Such a proposal was bound to stir
up some dissent because housing was the badge which,
before all others, signalled one's status. Phyllis Clarke,
who lived in an eminently respectable street in the
Dingle, remembers how she was warned about the
tenements at the end of her block in the 1940s:

The tenements were thought of as dens of iniquity.
They were rough people and if we went near them we'd
get in trouble. Brunswick Gardens was a place you
didn't go near – though I've heard some people say that
there were some nice people living in them.[9]

Far from being a barrier to Labour's electoral
progress, claims to respectability of this sort were
almost a condition of that progress. Labour's break-
through in Liverpool came before the First World War
and was made in districts of the city which had very
little connection with the port. Everton, Edge Hill and
St Annes, clustered around the inland edge of the city,
housed large numbers of skilled workers in manufacturing and service industries. Like other city wards,
they were densely populated and the equivalent of
medium-sized towns. In 1921 Everton had a

population of 36,000 people, which made it bigger than Jarrow, the Tyneside shipbuilding town; Edge Hill, with 34,500, was bigger than the London borough of Twickenham; St Annes, with 23,000, was the same size as Salisbury, Wiltshire's county town. The very size of the districts meant that they were not homogeneous but they did, on the other hand, have very distinct characteristics which quickly turned them into reliable places for Labour.

In the decade before the First World War the ferment of religious sectarianism was at its height in Liverpool politics and the critical point for the Tories was the extent to which they could play the Protestant card. In this respect, Edge Hill, Everton and St Annes were all unlikely places. In Edge Hill the Catholic population was very small and confined to one corner of the ward, well away from the respectable artisan terraces in which lived large numbers of skilled building workers of Welsh origin who belonged to Welsh-speaking chapels. Membership of these congregations insulated them from the sort of militant evangelism that typically defined Protestantism in Liverpool.[10] In Everton there was another Welsh colony with a Welsh Calvinist chapel, but Everton was also one of the very few districts of the city that housed large numbers of skilled and 'respectable' Catholics – whose vote Labour could be confident of in the absence of Irish Nationalist candidates. St Annes combined skilled Jewish workers in the furnishing and clothing trades with Irish Catholics working mainly in road transport.

Other features of these wards also made them likely places for Labour. Apart from the obvious benefits to Labour of a European socialist influence among the Jewish artisans of St Annes, there was the strength of the Co-operative movement in Everton and Edge Hill.

And given the occupational profile of both Everton and
Edge Hill, many workers would have been members of
the relevant craft unions. In short, and taking the
different features together, these wards had the kind
of socio-economic profile that was helping Labour to
win elections all over Britain. The profile of the wards
also reflected the general character of the Labour
Party in Liverpool. Like the Labour Party generally,
its members had drunk at the well of dissent,
Nonconformism and self-help. Of the seven Labour
councillors elected in 1911, six were trade union
officers and the seventh held a responsible position in
the Co-operative movement.

Many of the social and economic characteristics
present in Everton and Edge Hill were present also in
two wards adjacent to docklands – Kirkdale in the
North End and Dingle in the South. In each ward there
were skilled workers who were members of both the
Co-op and trade unions and had Nonconformist
affiliations – but Dingle stayed Tory until the 1930s
and Kirkdale until the 1940s. The Labour vote,
however, was very respectable even before the First
World War – on several occasions, Labour candidates
mustered between 30 and 40 per cent of the vote in
both wards in a straight fight with either Tory or
Protestant candidates. Labour's problems in these
wards were not so much with the respectable and
regularly employed as with other sections of the
electorate. The people of Dingle and Kirkdale had in
common their dependence on the port, but where the
'respectable' part of the populations had mainly skilled
and permanent jobs, another part of the population
consisted of the better-off sections of the casually
employed and regularly employed who had in their
working lifetime risen from casualism. These workers,
with a toe-hold in the older and cheaper artisan

terraces, were the ones who followed the Lodges on 12 July and who voted Tory in the local elections. Protestantism as a theology had little part to play in any of this. The Tories and their partners in the Protestant Party battened on the fear-fattened prejudices of people who were, at best, notional Protestants but who were very definitely opposed to the Irish Catholics who posed a constant threat to their marginal privileges in the casual labour markets.

After experiencing the full virulent flood of sectarianism during the 1910 General Election campaign in Kirkdale, Ramsay MacDonald is reputed to have said that: 'Liverpool is rotten and we had better recognise it.'[11] This was an accurate, if excessively brief, estimate. Sectarianism bedevilled Liverpool's politics to an extent unequalled anywhere else in mainland Britain – except Glasgow. It had been calculatingly used in the nineteenth century to keep the Liberals out of office and was used again to keep Labour out of office for more than half the twentieth century. In terms of the number of votes, sectarianism influenced relatively few non-Catholic voters by the end of the First World War, but there were nevertheless enough to turn the trick and maintain Tory control.

Sectarianism had as geat an impact on the developing style and character of the city Labour Party as it had on the outcome of elections. Labour inherited the Catholic wards after Irish independence led to the collapse of the Irish Nationalist Party. There was, however, a brief interregnum between the end of the Irish Nationalists and the takeover by Labour. In the 1920s the Irish Nationalist Party became a Catholic party, controlled by the archdiocese for the purposes of promoting Catholic interests. The new party did not survive changes in the local Roman Catholic hierarchy but it did mean that when Labour was at last adopted in the Catholic districts it only meant putting a different label on old machinery. Labour absorbed councillors who had been instruments of the church and it inherited organisations that knew more about clientelism, autocracy and priestly patronage than about the beliefs in democratic and constitutional procedures which were the hallmarks of the Labour Party and the 'respectable' working class. Although the Labour Party was now formally much larger, it was in practice two parties and the Catholic section, organised as a caucus, was dominant.

The Catholic faction was unaccustomed and indeed unsympathetic to ideas of a participating membership. It had a horse-trading approach to political organi- sation where things were arranged through nods, winks and favours done for friends, relatives and constituents. This method of operating at ward level became the method of the city party itself. In the mid-1950s, at the very time that Labour was coming to power in the city, its bedrock base in the Catholic wards of the other Liverpool was beginning to come apart. The parishes, so central to all social life, were being whittled down in size by clearances and undermined in influence by improvements in living standards. By the late 1960s party organisation had become so degenerate in the Catholic wards that it consisted of little more than the sitting councillors and small cliques of friends. Things were not noticeably better in the adjacent and largely non-Catholic wards that by then were reliably Labour. The political style of working brought into the Labour Party by relabelled but unreconstructed Irish Nationalists, and adopted by successive leaders, had so permeated the party that organisation almost everywhere was an empty shell. The party managed to stagger through the 1970s in this condition but before the end of that decade social and economic conditions had deteriorated very sharply and attention was turning to local politics. The Labour Party, just like a poorly run company, was ripe for a takeover.

There is no mystery – and neither was there anything notably improper – about the means used by the Militant Tendency to gain a toe-hold and then build a base in the Liverpool Labour Party. What is far less clear is how this sect, with a minority of members, nevertheless managed to win and then hold leading positions in the city council's Labour group. To this simple question there is only a complicated and several-sided answer, and it begins in a not very obvious place – in the nature of trade unionism among the casually employed workers of the other Liverpool.

Flurries of activity along the waterfront in the early 1890s provided a solid basis for permanent union organisation among dockers, seamen, carters, warehousemen and workers in mills and refineries. Membership was patchy and unstable, but it held on long enough to get a further boost in the five year period before the First World War. Growth continued during the war and accelerated until the collapse of the post-war boom early in 1921. The same sequence of union development was seen all over Britain, but in terms of numbers enrolled as members the figures were swollen in the ports where the system of casual labour, incapable of producing the 'loyal worker' phenomenon often found in the smaller factory towns, worked to the unions' advantage. While the figures in the following table should be treated with a great deal of suspicion, they are, nevertheless, suggestive of how quickly unions could grow in this period, especially after the successful strike of 1911.

Membership of the Liverpool Transport Workers Council Before and After the General Transport Strike, 1911

Occupation	May	November
General labourers	1,000	4,000
Sailors and Firemen	4,000	15,000
Cooks and Stewards	2,000	13,000
Warehouse and Millworkers	nil	3,500
Carters	5,500	7,500
Railwaymen	3,000	10,000
Navvies	1,000	4,000
Dockers	8,000	31,000

Source: *Liverpool Daily Post and Mercury*, 4 November 1911

As in previous periods of trade union growth, this phase saw the creation of many new local unions organising specific groups of workers. Typical of these were the Liverpool Upholstresses' Society and the Liverpool Waitresses' Society, but unions of this sort were too narrowly based to live much beyond the first flushes of enthusiasm. The real and lasting growth was among the bigger unions like the National Amalgamated Society of Sailors and Firemen or what were to become the giants after a series of mergers in the 1920s – the Transport and General (TGWU) and the General and Municipal Workers (NUGMW). Both came to have very large memberships in Liverpool and their influence in the city has always been considerable. It is not entirely coincidental that two of the best known national leaders of these unions in the period since 1945, Jack Jones and David Basnett, were Liverpudlians.

The big new unions were a response to the lack of co-ordination and impermanence of organisation that had hitherto characterised the trade unionism of semi- and unskilled workers. But the amalgamations came at a time when trade union membership in Britain was falling rapidly from 8,250,000 in 1920 to 5,500,000 in 1925. The TGWU, the NUGMW and other unions organising workers in industries quickly affected by trading recessions were immediately thrown on the defensive and organisational survival came to have the highest priority.

Survival called for a delicate balancing act in which unions could deliver disciplined membership to employers in order to persuade them to maintain, extend or newly enter into permanent national negotiating bodies. On the other hand the unions had to have some appearance of participatory democracy to retain the members' allegiance and to keep them from pursuing sectional interests to the point of undermining the employers' commitments to negotiating bodies. It was the second of these two performances which was the most difficult. It was also the one which stored up so much trouble for the unions in the post-war period and, incidentally, contributed so much to Liverpool's reputation as a leading centre of trade union militancy.

A precondition of participatory democracy in a trade union is the opportunity for local memberships to influence bargaining outcomes by making initiatives and by voting on agreements that have been tentatively made elsewhere. None of these conditions were met in the unions with substantial memberships on the Liverpool waterfront during the inter-war period or, indeed, during much of the post-war period either. From the 1920s until the 1960s local initiatives

were usually regarded as disruptive or even destruc-
tive, and tight central control of the union's govern-
mental machinery was believed essential. The formal
machinery and processes of democracy written into
rule books was no obstacle to central control in such
unions as the Sailors and Firemen or, its successor the
National Union of Seamen, and the TGWU. In these
unions, and without the formal constitution being
blatantly breached, unelected full-time officers who
were constitutionally civil servants were able to
control the formal processes of democracy.

The precise methods used to maintain control varied
according to the constitution of the union concerned,
although the general principles were identical.
Full-time officers, unlike lay members, were not
confined to one workplace nor to dealing with one
employer and low-level functionaries such as foremen.
The performance of the full-time officers job bestowed
a wider and deeper knowledge of internal union
politics and practices as well as a readier facility in
handling people and situations. Full-timers were
therefore in an extremely strong position effectively to
determine the membership of branch, district, regional
and executive committees. Where memberships were
constantly on the move, as in the seafarers' unions,
dominance by officials was almost total in the
inter-war years.

Effective membership participation was not only
short-circuited by the situational advantages of the
full-timer – the members themselves came poorly
equipped in the basic skills of citizenship. Very, very
few waterfront trade union members could have had
any knowledge or experience of organisational politics
or any opportunity to learn. Suffrage, itself the most
primitive and minimal form of democratic expression,
was heavily restricted for adult males until 1918 and

for women until 1928. In pre-First World War
Liverpool up to 60 per cent of adult males in docklands
were disenfranchised, and these were the very people
who were flooding into the TGWU. Merchant seamen,
for their part, could not register as absent voters and
were therefore almost wholly excluded from the
electorate. Political parties, friendly societies, working
man's clubs were the sort of places where workers
could gain some experience of participatory organisation – but these were the institutions of the
respectable working class rather than the casually
employed dockers and seamen. Semi- and unskilled
workers, furthermore, would not usually have
encountered the habits of deliberative thinking and
disciplined problem-solving required in learning and
pursuing a skilled trade. In short, the members of the
waterfront unions could bring with them little of the
experience relevant to running an organisation of any
kind. The lack of organisational experience was
compounded by casual employment: impermanence of
employment was inevitably coupled with erratic
payment of union subs, and a poorly developed sense of
the unions as being permanent organisations that
were *theirs*.

The seamen's union stood out as being the union
most blatantly under the control of officials. This
resulted as much from a closed-shop agreement made
with the shipowners at the end of the First World War
as from an absentee membership. The quid pro quo for
the employers' enforcement of union membership as a
condition of employment was that the union would
screen out 'undesirables', crush rebellions and generally encourage 'responsible' attitudes. The rhythm of
the seafaring life, however, ran quite contrary to neat
organisational requirements. The travelling life and
the tight cellular organisation of the ship's social

structure sustained a marked degree of independent-mindedness amongst seafarers as well as regular opportunity for exposure to the working class movements of other countries.

Before the First World War a number of Liverpool seamen who had deserted their ships in the USA became rank-and-file members of the anarcho-syndicalist Industrial Workers of the World, and a number of them returned to play leading parts in the Liverpool labour movement in the inter-war years. It is common knowledge that syndicalism came to Britain circuitously: instead of crossing the Channel from France, it came either across the Atlantic from the USA, or went from the USA to Australia and thence to Britain. In this as in other matters concerning the labour movement on Merseyside, there is little doubt that seamen played an important role in the transmission of ideas and information.[12]

Seafaring was a nursery of dissentient culture but the impact of dissidence was less on seafarers' trade unionism (though it was present and influential) than on the organisations in other trades. Seafarers regularly moved in and out of a range of land-based occupations and in their wake left traces of their experience and of their habits of mind. In post-war Liverpool, when autocracy came under steadily increasing attack, the direct and indirect influence of seamen was to be found everywhere.

The overwhelmingly prominent feature in British post-war trade union development has been the struggle of attrition against autocratic internal government. The timing of change within unions and between different industries has been extremely uneven but the *pattern* has been familiar and common: workplace trade union organisations have everywhere attempted to restrict or eliminate the influence of

national and local full-time officers. One of the
factory-based organisations in the vanguard of change
in the UK was at the Dunlop plant on Liverpool's
southern border. Fred Christopher, an active trade
unionist in the factory for nearly thirty years until its
closure in 1979, had a vivid recollection of the
difficulties he and his colleagues faced in the 1950s:

> There were always times when you'd go in to see the
> personnel manager with your tongue in your cheek a
> bit and you wouldn't worry too much about losing. But
> there were other issues where you knew very well you
> were on a winner – and then you'd come up against a
> blank wall. Often their idea then was that they thought
> we'd call in a full-timer and they knew from experience
> they'd get what they wanted out of him. That's why we
> always said that when we went 'outside' we lost it.[13]

The struggles for local autonomy had two main
features: a demand that nationally negotiated deals
should be referred back to local members for their
decision and a demand that full-time officers should
only have an advisory role in plant-level negotiations.
Liverpool workers were in the forefront of campaigns
within their unions to secure these objectives, and by
the end of the 1960s had secured enough success for
the city to acquire a reputation in trade union circles
as being a formidably well organised place. If this
reputation had some justification, the view of the city
as a place of notably strike-prone workers was wildly
misleading. The evidence of strikes on Merseyside is
substantial and pretty conclusive – taking one
industry with another, the region does not stand out as
being abnormal or unusual.[14]

More than anything else it was the *style* of Liverpool
trade unionists that attracted the attention – as much
from within the trade union movement as from

amongst employers and politicians. The sense of this is captured very neatly by Huw Beynon in his comparison of shop stewards from the Ford plants at Halewood and Swansea. At Halewood:

> The stewards were young men. They wore sharp clothes; suits with box jackets. They thought of themselves as smart, modern men; and this they were. They walked with a slight swagger, entirely alert and to the point of things. They walked, talked and looked as they were. They knew what their bit of the world was about and they were prepared to take on anybody who challenged it.

At Swansea:

> Their heritage was the pits. They carried the marks of the pit in blue on their hands and faces. Union men. The solid, traditional heart of the British labour movement. Home-knitted zipper cardigans – the occasional floral tie.[15]

These observations recall once more the mood of the 1960s. A mood which was brash, mocking and irreverent and which the Beatles were reckoned to express most eloquently. But the Beatles' manner of dress and way of presenting themselves was not borrowed from the times and its prevailing currents of sentiment. It was borrowed from the way of being themselves that was already established among self-respecting Liverpudlians. The Beatles were expressive of Liverpool before they were expressive of the 1960s. Nevertheless, the elevation of the Beatles to the status of folk heroes had its effects in Liverpool. Liverpudlians, already confident of being taller than anyone else, were now grown even higher.

Sharing in this process of creating and reinforcing the image of the ideal Liverpudlian as a person of

swagger and mickey-taking were the city's younger
trade unionists. But these were not the craft-proud
boilermakers and fitters or the craft-defensive shipwrights. These were the seamen and dockers, the
workers in the big factories on the city's perimeter who
had been rehoused in the fringe estates. The clearance
of worn out dockland housing, the expansion of
manufacturing industry and nearly full employment
helped spread the character of the other Liverpool
right across the city and even beyond, into the new
towns of Runcorn and Skelmersdale.[16]

Taking all of the various elements together, it is easy
to see why Liverpool should have been in the forefront
of trade union reform. The vast nature of its casual
labour force and its dominance of the local labour
market provided Liverpool's workers with a more
concentrated experience of undemocratic trade unionism than could be found anywhere else in Britain. But
the moment for this form of trade union practice had
passed and working against it were a range of factors.
There were the men back from the war at sea and in
the services expecting to find a new and more
egalitarian society and who were impatient of
obstacles. There was the dramatic reduction in the
degree to which casual employment really was casual.
There were the rising expectations of continuing
improvements in standards of living. There were the
established and self-confident traditions of the other
Liverpool only waiting, as it were, to be liberated. And
then came rock'n'roll and its social subversiveness
which Liverpool, with its long standing American
associations and its democratic temperament, drank
down in quarts.

The willing trade union rebels of the 1960s were the
very first generation of young Liverpudlians to have
grown up with the ability to move easily from one job to

another. And nowhere was this newly conferred economic independence so available as amongst seafarers. As early as 1951, for example, 37,000 British seamen had given up the sea while 38,000 replacements (50 per cent of them with previous maritime experience) had been recruited.[17]

We have already seen that seafarers had always nurtured a view of themselves as being free men who would never be bound to one ship for more than one voyage – but in previous times of more men than berths, the self-image had in it more of the wish than the fulfillment. In the post-war years and as late as the mid-1970s rhetoric and reality became interchangeable. Emlyn Williams, who began his career at sea in the early 1970s on a transatlantic liner, soon learned how easy it was to move around:

> There used to be three of us shipping out together, and we could get jobs with no trouble. I remember one time we paid off the *Cotopaxi* on a Friday afternoon, stayed in Liverpool over the weekend, went down to the Pool on Monday morning and were sailing out at Monday teatime. Then it was no trouble. Sometimes I'd just go home for a few days, then I'd come back, have a look around and ship out again. It was easy then, wasn't it? You could just pick and choose your ship and go where you wanted.[18]

This degree of independence, however, when taken together with the magnitude of labour turnover in the industry, severely hampered those activists intent on the reform of the seafarers' union.

It is impossible to overstate the bitter contempt in which seamen held their union in the 1940s, 1950s and most of the 1960s. For years, and with only few exceptions, they had seen their officials board their ships on return to the UK and go first to visit the master to drink his whisky and enquire after the behaviour of the crew. They had also seen their national officers negotiate agreements, in what was then a relatively prosperous industry, which left them almost as badly paid as farm-workers.

Anger and frustration had naturally run higher in Liverpool than anywhere else and the centre of organised opposition was bound to be in the city. Well before the Second World War the union's head office looked balefully upon Liverpool as the focal point for dissidence and these well justified suspicions did not abate after the war. A major unofficial strike in 1947, after the union had agreed to a wage reduction, was organised from Liverpool and led to the jailing of two of its leaders. In the 1950s and 1960s Liverpool was the home-base of the opposition movement – the National Seamen's Reform Movement. Further unofficial strikes – in 1955 and 1960 – were again organised from Liverpool and, yet again, strike leaders were jailed.

By 1966 the Reform Movement's persistence, its ingenuity in maintaining its organisation and credibility among union members generally, was at last rewarded – they finally had a majority on the national executive and an official strike was called. In 1975, Joe Kenny, leading Reform Movement member from Liverpool and Harold Wilson's *bête noire* in the 1966 strike, became the National Union of Seamen's national organiser. It had taken the seamen more than a quarter of a century to reform their union, to rid it of corrupt and incompetent officials and then to introduce a system of balloting members no matter where they were in the world. It was a terrible and tragic irony that no sooner had the Liverpool seamen played a leading role in turning their union into an enviable model of democratic practice than their port underwent rapid decline and their industry tottered ever nearer to total collapse.[19]

Seamen who went ashore to work in factories, in the docks, on the construction sites, took with them their experience of the unreformed NUS and a thoroughly jaundiced expectation that every other union would be as bad. Few other unions were as rotten as the old NUS, although TGWU members on the docks, for example, were locked into endless conflicts with their full-time officers because there was no formally recognised system of trade union representation on the quays or down below in the hatches.

The docks section of the TGWU had a large corps of full-time officers who were supposed to represent the members in the branches. This made a rough kind of sense when work was genuinely casual – but not after the war when the casual element was greatly reduced even though far from eliminated.[20] There is no doubt that the persistence of 'officer-power' in the docks, where it was foolishly supported by the employers, was a continuing source of aggravation and served only to inflame the in-built explosive potential of casualism.[21]

Casualism, the scattering of dockers over a huge area, the plethora of employers (115 in 1962 but down to 13 after decasualisation), the priests on the shoulders of some of the full-time officers and general Catholic meddling in branch affairs, the long standing rivalries between North and South Ends with Protestant versus Catholic undertones ... There were just too many sources of division among dockers for them to have produced a united front and forced the employers to recognise their own representatives. But their robust independence contributed powerfully to working-class Liverpudlians' sense of themselves, and the full emotional, cultural and political force of this was movingly reflected in the plays by Neville Smith and Jim Allen shown on television in the 1960s and in Alan Bleasdale's plays produced for stage and television in the 1970s and 1980s.[22]

The unrivalled trade union showpiece in Liverpool was the Dunlop factory mentioned earlier. Purpose-built in the late 1930s as a aircraft factory at a time of rapid rearmament, the plant was taken over by Dunlop at the end of the war and was soon producing, under the one vast roof, a range of tyres and tubes for vehicles, rubber footwear and an assortment of other heavy rubber goods. Already, in the late 1950s, the factory had an unusually sophisticated trade union organisation and was the national centre of opposition within the UK rubber industry to the conduct of negotiations by national officers who were not then obliged to refer deals back to the members. The initiative for the formation of a national combine committee to advance the claims of rank-and-file members came from Liverpool, and the story is told here by Fred Christopher:

The combine came about because we wanted a lay delegate on the National Joint Industrial Council. There was just no way the full-timers were going to have that and we fought it for a long time. There were times when a number of us had our shop stewards' credentials withdrawn by the union. To give you some idea of how bad they were, we asked the union to give us some finance so that we could have the meeting in the Stork Hotel. No way, they said, there's just no way. Then the word got about that we were trying to form a breakaway union. We weren't, but even so that was the word that got around. Then, in the *Manchester Guardian* on the Monday morning there was an article naming me and Stan, Charlie, Bill Parry and Alec Roberts. The article said that while we weren't Trotskyites, that we were trying to form a breakaway union. We never knew where that story came from but it must have been somebody in the T and G.

We had to finance that meeting by putting a penny a week levy on the membership. Instead of paying 8d a

week the men paid 9d and the women paid 6d instead
of 5d. It added up to quite a lot of money because there
were 7,000 people there then. People came up from
Avon, Michelin, Goodyear, Pirelli and of course from
other Dunlop plants.[23]

Paranoid reactions by the powerful to threats from
below are normal, and at this plant had been
anticipated and allowed for. The activists' response to
opposition was to 'invade' the official machinery by
placing their nominees in the governing structure of
the TGWU at district, regional and national levels. So
successful was this tactic that by the late 1960s a
senior shop steward was both regional chair and a
member of the union's General Executive Council. At
the time of the factory closure he had become national
president of the TGWU and a General Council member
of the TUC. Another of the senior shop stewards and
the leading 'architect' at the plant had also become a
member of the General Executive Council.

In the early 1970s, and again accurately reading
developments, the Liverpool plant organised a token
international strike of Dunlop-Pirelli workers in the
UK, France, Italy and Spain. (This strike is
commemorated in a bronze plaque on the speakers'
podium at the Pierhead – the casting made by Arthur
Dooley, sculptor and ex-Dunlop worker.) After this
strike international conferences and exchanges
became regular, and during the campaign of resistance
against closure in 1979 French and Italian delegations
arrived to address a mass meeting.

Not much more than a mile away from the Dunlop
factory – and much closer given the exchange of
personnel – was the new Ford factory, just over the city
border at Halewood, a previously insignificant village.
Dunlop organisation was seen as a model by several
young workers who had served 'apprenticeships' there

and who very rapidly rose to prominence at Ford's. The docks apart, it was events at Ford's which more than anything else helped Liverpool acquire its militant reputation. Ford workers were translated into *Liverpool* workers and so when, for example, the press discovered an exiled Liverpudlian at the head of the Pilkington strike in 1970, a front page headline shouted 'SCOUSE POWER'. The fact that almost anything Liverpool was 'news' in the 1960s contributed to the attention that Ford workers received – and a bonus for the media were the shop-floor representatives who were certain to supply pithy and slightly sarcastic, tongue-in-cheek replies to pushy young interviewers sent up from London.

Unnoticed by the media, when it reported on the Ford plant at Halewood, was the severely damaged trade union organisation at Dagenham which left untenanted the leadership of Ford UK workers. Played down or misunderstood was the foolishness of Ford management in trying to exclude the TGWU from organising in a factory which was in a well-known 'T and G town'. Unmentioned were the southerners brought in as supervisors. Of all the blunders made by Ford's management when it came to Liverpool, this was one of the worst. Commenting on the arrogance of Dagenham supervisors sent to Halewood, one of the senior shop stewards said:

> They thought they could treat us like dirt ... We were just dirty Scousers who'd crawled in off the docks out of the cold. We'd never even seen a car plant before and those sods had been inside one since they were knee-high. We took a hammering.[24]

An earlier generation at Dunlop had encountered a similar problem – Fred Christopher said they had:

... noticed that all the senior management came from Brum. They treated us like colonials; they had a real settler outlook. We were just the bloody 'no marks'. All this made us into militants.[25]

In truth, nothing exceptional happened at Halewood. Nothing that was being pushed there was not being pushed everywhere else. At Halewood they wanted shop-floor representation on the National Joint Negotiating Committee; they wanted deals to be ratified by the workers in the plants; and more generally, they wanted proper procedures on the shop-floor to eliminate the arbitrary exercise of power over individuals by managers and supervisors. These sorts of ambitions were being pursued throughout industry and were wholly attuned to a period in which people sought optimistically for modernity and progress. To be modern and progressive meant discarding 'tradition' – and that, in turn, usually required a dissolving of the grossnesses of hierarchy and an embracing of the spirit (but not usually the substance) of egalitarianism. In the 1960s there was an atmosphere which hinted at the possibility of the world being turned upside down. Not so much a world where the poor would be rich and the rich poor. Merely a place where first intuition presumed that one person, regardless of rank, was as good as another.

In the other Liverpool such generous intuitions were already established and proclaimed regularly in the now widely diffused and liberal style of the returning seafarer. But this generosity of outlook was frightening in its implications to those whose power and status was being disturbed. When in the 1970s and 1980s the economic and cultural outlook turned sourer and meaner, the industrial expression of the natural democracy of Liverpudlians was getting to be defined as a form of blight equivalent to the nineteenth-century Irish potato famine.

Liverpool and its region had undergone fifteen unrelenting years of factory closures and rising unemployment by the time Derek Hatton and his Militant colleagues came to national prominence in 1983. A full two-thirds of the dock system lay silent and inert and the ferries no longer needed to weave in and out of river traffic and dodge around the stern of a ship swinging to the tide. Factories that had brought hopes of a broader based and more secure economy had closed one by one, and firms adapting to technological change halved and then halved again their workforces. In docklands, even though 75 per cent of the population had been scattered to new estates and new towns, unemployment rates rose as high as 60 per cent for those left behind.

Although Liverpool was not a place where self-respecting people could think of defeat without first putting up a fight, reaction to economic decline was nevertheless slow to develop. And when it did come no one would have predicted a leading role for one of the many and marginal Trotskyist sects, even though the Labour Party was bankrupt in ideas and organisation.

Militant was established in several of the more degenerate ward and constituency Labour Parties in the city by the late 1970s, and this helped give it legitimacy and credibility with younger trade unionists who had grown up in a climate of expectations where a win or a draw seemed more certain than a defeat. It was the militancy of Militant that impressed, not the deep-laid, apocalyptic strategies. Most trade unionists were too busy in their unions and too accustomed to thinking in terms of limited and achievable objectives to be skilled – or even interested – in the theological coils of left sectarianism.

While it was background trade union support and encouragement that helped Militant to prominence, it was also trade union withdrawal of support and encouragement that brought Militant down. Long before the Labour Party and the law lords had expelled Militant from the Labour Party and the Town Hall respectively, the trade unions had refused to allow their members to be used as an instrument in a political confrontation with the government. In Liverpool's social character there was a pride in a readiness to fight but there was never, ever the slightest hint of a belief in self-destruction.

Notes

1 Quoted in Mervyn Jones, 'The Dangerous City – Liverpool's History of Social Disorder', unpublished paper from the 'Conference of Three Cities', Université de Paris VIII, March 1987.
2 Stan Coulthard, retired Communist Party Liverpool organiser, in an interview with the author, January 1973.
3 Hawthorne, op. cit., p.13.
4 Quoted in M.B. Simey, op. cit., p.100.
5 Liverpool Economic and Statistical Society, *How the Casual Labourer Lives*, Liverpool 1909, pp. xxvi-xxvii.
6 Orchard, op. cit., p.659.
7 Sir Joseph Cleary, ex-Labour councillor, in an interview with the author, April 1978.
8 *Liverpool Daily Post*, 7 July 1908.
9 Phyllis Clarke (pseudonym), secretary of a South Liverpool community association, in an interview with the author, May 1978.
10 For the Welsh in Liverpool, see R. Merfyn Jones and D. Ben Rees, *Liverpool Welsh and Their Religion*, Liverpool 1984.
11 Quoted in H. Pelling, *A Social Geography of British Elections, 1885–1910*, London 1967, p.252.
12 See Tony Lane, 'A Merseysider in Detroit', *History Workshop Journal*, No.11, 1981, pp.139-40.
13 Fred Christopher, ex-foreman, Dunlop's, in an interview with the author, 11 June 1979.
14 See R. Bean and P. Stoney, 'Strikes on Merseyside: A Regional

Analysis', *Industrial Relations Journal*, No.1, 1986.

15 Huw Beynon, *Working for Ford*, Harmondsworth 1973, pp.80-1.

16 By 1961 Liverpool City Council had entered into overspill agreements involving a total of more than 100,000 people with Ellesmere Port (20,000), Skelmersdale (37,500), Runcorn (30,000), Widnes (14,000) and Winsford (1,600).

17 *Fairplay*, 3 May 1951.

18 Quoted in T. Lane, *Grey Dawn Breaking*, p.165.

19 For an account of developments in the NUS, see A.P. Wailey, 'Storm from Liverpool: British Seamen and their Union, 1920–1970'. unpublished Ph.D. Thesis, University of Liverpool, 1985.

20 Average labour requirements on the docks still varied considerably. If in peak years 95 per cent of the labour force was hired, it went as low as 79 per cent in slump years. The overall average for 1954–1965 was only eighty-four per cent. See R. Lawton and C.M. Cunningham (eds), *Merseyside: Social and Economic Studies*, London, 1970.

21 The employers often had only themselves to blame for the strikes they complained of. By their short-sighted insistence on propping up the system of full-time union officers, they delayed the inevitable introduction of the far more rational system of workplace representation.

22 Neville Smith, *After a Lifetime*, Jim Allen, *The Big Flame*, Alan Bleasdale, *Down the Dock Road* and *The Boys from the Blackstuff*.

23 Fred Christopher interview, loc.cit.

24 Quoted in Beynon, op. cit., p.87.

25 Fred Christopher interview, loc. cit.

5 Arrival and Departure

There was more than a dash of bombast in the rhetoric used by the old families to extol the imperial and world role of Liverpool. But when they sold their firms, dissolved their local associations and enthusiastically assimilated themselves into the national elite, they left their grand words behind, lodged in the mentalities of the local people. The people of Liverpool, especially those of the other Liverpool, continued firm in their belief that their city was different and very definitely superior. The swagger came from the cultural aspects of an unusually large and highly developed seaport economy of long standing, but the rhetoric was borrowed and deployed to say something about the people of the other Liverpool in the same way that the

old families had used it to say something about
*them*selves.

The beliefs about Liverpool long outlived the
material conditions that had produced and sustained
them. This was neither irrational nor unusual. Any
Liverpudlian over the age of twenty-one who knew the
docks and river can remember the apparent confusion
of the movements of ships and cargoes. The bottom fell
out of the port economy too suddenly and with too little
counteracting economic compensation for there to be
any easy collective psychological adjustment to the
brutal fact that Liverpool no longer mattered in the
world, that the city's time had passed.

When the Militant-dominated Labour Party took
control in the Town Hall the real politics of the
programme went completely over the heads of all but
handfuls of those Liverpudlians familiar with left
sectarianism. The people of Liverpool were as un-
familiar with the doctrinal certainties of Trotskyism as
they were with those of the Mormons or Professor
Minford at Liverpool University. On the other hand,
the bombast of Militant was often received with some
sympathy – not necessarily for its content but certainly
for its tone. It asserted what Liverpudlians knew to the
very depths of their being – that this was a great city
and its people were not the sort to be trifled with.

In the middle of the noise was Derek Hatton, the
media's most favoured representation of Militant.
Derek Hatton was noticed less for his words than for
his persona. In this respect, if in no other, he would
have been identified by the more Whiggish of the old
families as a typically assertive *arriviste*. Among his
contemporaries in the general public he could be seen,
with some warmth of recognition, as a Cunard Yank
who seemed to have strayed into the Town Hall.
Noticing the flamboyance of dress and presentation of

self, it was hard to resist the belief that born twenty years earlier he would have been a waiter in the tourist class on the *Carinthia* or one of her sister ships. In Derek Hatton's style and accents Liverpool had turned full circle. The other Liverpool had at last arrived in the Town Hall. The tragedy of the arrival was not that it had happened but in the manner and timing of it. In the manner of its coming it was unfortunate that it should arrive dressed in the politics of impossibilism – that nothing in Liverpool, or indeed anywhere else, could be changed fundamentally until Britain had been cleansed by a revolution and then remade anew. The timing was a disaster. The city's original economic *raison d'être* had withered and many of the later economic graftings had fallen early victim to a recession worsened in the 1980s by excesses in Downing Street and Westminster. The other Liverpool arrived in a Town Hall still grand and almost unbelievably opulent in its inherited architecture and interior decoration and furnishing but dependent on Whitehall for revenue.

The end of Militant was the end of an era that had had only the briefest moment in office. The whole era from the mid-1960s to the mid-1980s was one of contradictions that were not usually obvious to outsiders. Outsiders noticed the native delight in hamming up the irreverence and the opposing and did not pick up the secret hopes of the people for a better society. Liverpudlians held their dreams close to their chests and even then mocked themselves for having them. After all, what historical experiences had they enjoyed which could sustain a conviction that the world might be changed for the better? The humour that Liverpudlians congratulate themselves on having is relevant here. It is the equivalent of spitting defiantly in the face of adversity and a refusing to accept the pessimism they often feel.

There is still enough of Liverpool's past imprinted in the character of younger generations to ensure that the swagger, the generosity, the independent-mindedness will survive into the foreseeable future. The city, meanwhile, will continue to change into a different place. So far as change is concerned, Liverpool has now rounded the corner by turning its back on the past. The port may not shrink any further and might actually grow – but not to its former size. Liverpool's future lies in being a different place and not in trying to be again what it was before. The city needed to get over its past before it could begin to think about its future, and the Militant phase hastened this process.

In some of the earlier decades of the nineteenth century Thomas Carlyle wrote of the destruction of Northern England by the smoke, soot and cinder of satanic mill chimneys. A latter-day Carlyle will soon be writing of comparable pollution of South-Eastern and Eastern England. The Garden of Kent turned into a huge car park and railway siding for cross-Channel traffic and the rest of the Home Counties made impossible by the density of people crushing in to look for the jobs squeezed out of the North. The more affluent, looking as always for some semi-sylvan, tidy and sterilised version of rural life, will push ever deeper into Hampshire, Oxfordshire and Suffolk only to be confronted by tens of thousands of others looking for the same thing.

Early in the twenty-first century horrified Northern viewers will be seeing videotapes in which the metropolis and the South-East are portrayed as a rat-maze of a modern urban hell. Life in Liverpool meanwhile, but also in Newcastle and Sheffield, Leeds and Bradford (and possibly even in Manchester), will be extraordinarily civilised. Relieved of over-densely populated acres, these will be spacious, open cities of

tree-lined streets, coppiced corners and wooded
hollows, teeming with wildlife where tenements and
tower blocks once stood.

Of all the Northern cities, Liverpool will be reckoned
the richest. It will be celebrated for the completeness of
its range of Victorian and Edwardian architecture, for
its unrivalled concentration of neo-Grecian public
buildings, for its art treasures and museums, for its
playwrights and poets, its artists and musicians. An
exciting city of light and colour and vitality produced
by a people proud of this, the first real garden city on
the bank of a river that surges with the tide to make a
vast inland lake.

The de-industrialisation of the late twentieth
century has brought the first possibility of creating
real garden cities rather than the toy-town suburbs of
Welwyn and Letchworth which trade falsely under the
name. Liverpool, with its superb endowment of river
and undulating terrain, its chain of parkland cutting
through the city, its electric social history and its
thriving cultural life will make York and Chester look
as prettily twee as they actually are.

Liverpool's first new future will be as one of the new
cultural capitals of Northern Europe. Its second new
future will be as a city of sophisticated, environ-
mentally sympathetic industries, of workshops known
for the excellence of their products and the originality
of their design. In becoming this place, long admiring
readers of William Morris's *News from Nowhere* will
recognise the realisation of his ambitions. And they
will think that Liverpool could hardly have been a
better place for it. Morris's ideal garden city was
populated by independent-minded people for whom
democracy was an essential precondition of a civilised
way of life.

Index